Journey to the Eye of the Heart

A Spiritual Odyssey of Hope, Faith and Love

Journey to the Eye of the Heart

A Spiritual Odyssey of Hope, Faith, and Love

Marcia Sutton

Journey to the Eye of the Heart
© 2012, 2022 by Marcia Sutton

WiseWoman Press
Vancouver, Washington, U.S.A.

www.wisewomanpress.com

ISBN: 978-0-945385-38-7

This book is graciously dedicated
to those beloveds who have
the eyes to see,
the ears to hear,
and the hearts to feel.

Contents

Foreword	i
Introduction - Into the Essence of Love	1
Chapter 1: Beginnings	7
The Forest	7
Chapter 2: Boundaries	19
The GreatWall	19
Chapter 3: Prayer	29
The MountainTop	29
Chapter 4: Meditation	45
The Convent	45
Chapter 5: Belief	55
The Concorde	55
Chapter 6: Surrender	59
The Mosque	59
Chapter 7: Gratitude	77
The Cathedral	77
Chapter 8: Sorrow	87
Mary's House	87
Chapter 9: Communion	103
The Upper Room	103
Chapter 10: Peace	115
The Poolside Mass	115
Chapter 11.	Love 121
The Ashram	121

Chapter 12: Joy	**125**
The Cave	125
Practices to Ease the Way	127
Spiritual Mentor	127
Prayer Partnering	127
Writing A Sacred Covenant	128
Starting A Christ Circle	128
An Uplifting Treatment	129
An Uplifting Treatment for Oneself	130
Prayer of Acceptance	131
Prayer of Reconciliation	132
About the Author	**133**
Acknowledgments	**135**
Gratitudes from Students & Colleagues	**137**
Publishers Note	**141**

We shall not cease from exploration
And the end of all our exploring
Will be to arrive where we started
And know the place for the first time.
~ T.S. Eliot

We travel initially to lose ourselves;
And we travel next, to find ourselves.
~ Pico Iyer

Foreword

I'm grateful for all who will be served by what has been written in this book. It fills me with joy to share it with others. My journey through the writing of this book has expanded my life in ways that I couldn't have known when I began this project. I share it with you in hopes that the great Joy I have gained from writing it blesses your own lives in glorious ways.

With Gratitude,

Rev. Dr. Marcia Sutton

Journey to the Eye of the Heart

"And he that set upon the throne said, Behold I make all things new. And he said unto me, Write, for I am giving you words that are true and faithful."
~Revelation 21:5

Purpose: LOVE

Vision: Writing in the Anointing of Christ

I am graciously accepting Christ's guidance and inspiration in the writing of this book.

I am expanding the expression of Love through every word that is written.

I am easily mastering any research and computer skills that will support the completion of this project.

I am being blessed with an abundance of time, money and support for this project.

I am entering into relationship with a publisher who fully supports this book for its divine right publication and distribution.

I am experiencing the ease of Christ in all negotiations and contract agreements.

I am knowing that everyone associated with the publication of this book is being blessed and prospered according to Jesus Christ.

~ *Marcia Sutton 10-28-12*

Introduction - Into the Essence of Love

As the opening quotes suggest, travel provides us the opportunity to broaden our perspective of life and teaches us about ourselves. This has certainly been true for me. To date, I've visited almost fifty countries and the experiences from some of these trips form the introductory stories that open each of the chapters of this book. My intention is to use my world travels as guideposts to share about the extraordinary invisible passage that led me into the inner realms of consciousness.

Many books have addressed the worldly path of the hero's journey. Still others have explored the dynamics of self-actualization for success in the world. This one is a record of my personal journey of self-realization into the essence of Love. It's about how I heard and answered the call of the Divine. It's about how I was led into places in awareness I never even knew existed. It's a journey that took me around the world and deep into the cave of my own heart.

Essentially, this book records my path to God. Its purpose is to share with you my journey from the seemingly "accidental" experiences of the existence of God to knowing the Divine as a living reality within my own being. It outlines my journey from the darkness of ignorance and unconsciousness to the Light of truth and wisdom. It exposes the rigors of beginning and sustaining a daily-dedicated spiritual practice. It shows how seeming failures often become the seeds for future success. It's also about knowing and experiencing the blessings of the promises of God that have been given in all the holy scriptures. Most importantly, it's about the inner journey that has been taken by the saints, sages, monks and holy ones from every spiritual tradition who have gone before us. These blessed individuals have led the way so that we may walk in their footsteps today.

The world's sacred traditions often speak of being "called" to a relationship with God. I have come to see that this call is not limited to a few select people nor is it just meant for priests, pastors, rabbis, imams, nuns, and monks. The call of the Divine is for every soul to know the truth of their being. A person's essential self is what becomes unveiled on the journey into the sacred center of their being. In the Eastern religious traditions, it's been known as the path of Enlightenment and in the West, it's often referred to the path of Illumination. Both ways lead us to this simple truth: The Light of the Divine is for all eternity and the Love of God is for all people.

This sacred call is what brought Arjuna to be in the chariot with Lord Krishna to have one of the most famous conversations in history. Today we know it as the *Bhagavad-Gita* (Song of God) of the Hindus and it teaches us about the authentic work of spiritual practice. It's the call that led the Buddha to follow the ascetics in the forest so he could "wake up," then sit beneath a fig tree to find how we, too, might come to see through the illusions of our minds and the passions of our senses. It's the call that brought Moses to Mt. Sinai to reveal the laws that, even today, deliver us from bondage. It's the call that took Mohammed to a cave on Mt. Hera so that we might know the importance of surrender as revealed by the Angel Gabriel. Finally, it's the call that delivered Jesus to Jerusalem so that humanity would be set free from the curse of the belief in death, forevermore.

The stories of the call to the Light in the lives of these great ones have guided humanity in untold ways. The call has come across all time, history and space to announce itself anew to us today.

This book tells the story of my calling and how I was led around the world only to discover and embrace its answer from within. Drawing from sacred writings as well as my own stories, you will be guided in seeing and experiencing the road map of this inner path. The journey in and of itself has been the real gift of my own walk. It has also served the lives of the blessed others who have been my companions on the way.

Nothing is ever wasted on the road of life. Everything in the outer world--every experience, encounter, circumstance, difficulty and challenge--can be used to reveal who we are at the center-most part of our being. To use them, we must develop the eyes to see, the ears to hear and the hearts to feel what is being graciously given to us from the invisible side of life. In this way, and only in this way, can every experience then become a marker on an individually designed roadmap home to one's 'true' self, the self that I call the 'Christ' within each one of us.

On the inner path, I have taken what appeared to be detours and discovered they were but shortcuts of sorts. Also, many planned timesaving steps took me into deep caverns of uncertainty and dread. Sometimes I have faced the most challenging and heartbreaking experiences only to later understand that those very experiences were necessary to develop the courage that would be needed later down the road.

You see, everything that happened to me was necessary for what was to be revealed down the road on the journey. Ultimately, these experiences had very little to do with the outer circumstances, the other people involved or the pains, disappointments and even successes I came to know. Instead, they had everything to do with bringing forth something from within me that had to be prepared and developed before I could make further progress.

Along the way, I found that what we are being taught or shown on the journey of self-exploration is often very simple. Sometimes it's about learning to accept where we find ourselves at any given phase in our lives. Sometimes it's about discovering the courage to forgive, especially those whom we love the most. Sometimes it's trusting that our needs will be met. Sometimes it's about yielding or slowing down. Most often, it's about learning how to love.

Finally, I now see that the call for me to walk in the footsteps of the ancient sages, saints, and masters couldn't be denied. Those precious words of God to Moses in the Egyptian desert at Mount Sinai became an ever-unfolding invitation for my journey: "Take off your sandals, the place where you are standing is holy ground." (Exodus 3:5).

Today, I know that all ground is holy when we walk in the Light of God's Love. I know and trust that each of us is always being uniquely guided to this holy place of illumined inner seeing. Our paths may look very different on the outer level but our destination is the same.

Beyond their differences, all the traditions teach the importance of spiritual practice, and all of them have developed a variety of practices to support their followers on the journey. Some of these practices will be introduced at various places in this book.

This is my journey from a pine forest in Michigan to the Temple of Light within my soul. It's a journey that took me to the eye of my own heart. I am grateful to be able to share it with you. I am also filled with joy in knowing deep within myself that this Light is the promise and ultimate destiny for every human being.

I now invite you to come with me into these sacred inner realms of awareness. May the gift of reading this book open new doors of perception on your path to the Light. May it serve to sustain, nurture, and guide you as you answer its call for your own spiritual odyssey.

I bless you, fellow traveler, as we journey to the Light of Divine Radiance that is the infinite, invisible presence that I call God.

Chapter 1: Beginnings

The Forest

Grayling, Michigan

Feeling tired from all the activity with my high school friends during a weekend of canoeing, I was grateful as we stopped to visit the Chapel in the Woods situated deep within a pine forest in the upper part of lower Michigan.

Getting off the bus, most of my friends followed our teacher/chaperones into the chapel. I started to follow the group but realized that I simply wanted some time to myself. Off the chapel area, I found a side path winding its way into the woods.

As I started down the path, I was overcome by how good it felt to simply be alone. I paused and recalled the famous poem I had recently memorized for a class lesson, Robert Frost's "The Road Less Traveled." It seemed as if, for these short few minutes, I was on my own less-traveled road.

Then it happened, just as St Paul had said it would - in the "twinkling of an eye." (1 Corinthians 15:52) I stopped and stood, transfixed.

Silence.

The sun was breaking through as my gaze traveled up the tall trees with their elegant green arms reaching to the bright blue sky. I was fully connected to everything around me. There was a feeling of peace and love beyond any I had ever known. At that moment I knew that I was part of something much greater than just myself.

Here I was, standing in the real chapel of God's glorious universe, and I was part of it--not separate from it. In this holy encounter, time itself ceased and I knew and sensed God as a living reality.

I don't know the exact beginning of my walk with God but I do know that during that experience in the woods I realized that God walked with me. Today, I am more sure in my use of the word "God," but back then in high school, I wasn't. I fumbled over it or, for the most part, kept it secret. But that day was very different from my life before.

I didn't fully understand what happened to me on that wooded path and I couldn't even begin to explain it. Yet, I knew--in that eternal moment--that I had experienced myself as part of all life.

Little did l comprehend that it would take some thirty years, many obstacles, and numerous detours to understand the truth of that experience for myself. It's as if I had been given a "peek" into the reality of existence, only to discover that I would have to build the chapel in my own heart in order to consciously return to the sense of eternal oneness that I had known for that brief moment in the forest. I was in awe that day—in awe of the majesty and beauty of God's expression.

The purpose of this book is to share with you my journey from this seemingly "accidental" experience of the existence of God to knowing It as a living reality within my own consciousness. I have come to realize that there has never been a time when I have walked outside the Presence of Divine Love. Of course, conditions, appearances, and the circumstances of life made it *seem* as if God was always far away, but I learned otherwise. My journey to the "eye of the heart" is a journey through all those life experiences into the center of Divine Love itself.

If I count that walk in the woods as one of the great markers on my spiritual path, another of my early memories forms the foundation for many of my worldly experiences. One of my significant childhood recollections is of standing at the big picture window in our living room in Lansing, Michigan. Looking out of it, I saw my beloved grandparents waving good-bye to us as their car backed out of the driveway. This was the beginning of what would become their annual trips out west for the winter. My grandfather had been diagnosed with emphysema and was advised to get out of the cold Michigan winters. For nearly a year, they had been saving money so they could spend the coldest part of our winter with old friends who were now living in sunny Southern California.

It was a sad time for me. I couldn't imagine how long they would have to be gone. I even feared they might not return. I loved them so much. In their leaving, I felt a loss that would be with me in one form or another for many years to come.

There was also another feeling. Actually, the feeling was a decision I made standing at that window, watching my grandparents drive away. Somewhere in me, I knew I would go to California, too. In fact, I made the decision that I would go to other places, too: places I was just learning about in school and seeing on our new black-and-white television screen.

Later, as the horizons of my world expanded, my list of destinations did as well. These places and things I added to my list to see would eventually take me around the world.

Much to my relief and happiness, my grandparents did return the following spring, before my April birthday. And, oh, what a reunion it was! They brought us stuff we had never seen, such as avocados, and Grandma cooked exotic new dishes like Spanish rice. They had even bought a fancy mixer called an Osterizer in which we concocted all sorts of drinks, using foods we had never dreamed of eating in liquid form. They also brought back the best dresses for my sisters and me. These dresses became my favorites. They were more colorful and beautiful than anything that could be found in our relatively small city.

But that was not all. Shortly after they unpacked and settled back into the routine of daily life, the whole family, and even the neighbors, gathered to see the color slides my grandfather had taken of their trip. It is almost too trite to say that my eyes "bugged out" by all that I was seeing on the screen in their living room. Here I was, this young girl viewing sunsets that were beyond description, along with scenes of red dirt and rock formations taken along the Arizona highways. Through those slide shows, I also learned that the desert had flowers and that water that was dammed up could form beautiful lakes. And, oh, those fuchsias colored flowers crawling up the side of their friend's house! The oranges growing on the trees in the backyard where my grandparents were living while in California even looked bigger and brighter than those at our local grocery store.

I remember wanting to see those slides over and over again.

Most importantly, I remember my grandparents' pride for what they had done together. Like the spirit of the early pioneers before them, they had packed up their light green Ford and left their known world. They followed the map directions to US Highway Route #66, which then carried them due west—all the way to the Pacific Ocean.

The greatest thing is that they came back to share it all with me.

That's how I felt. Then, in the ensuing years of my young life, I watched them plan their yearly trips. I watched them save their dimes from each day's pocket change and put them in the little bank on top of their bedroom dresser. Everyone in the family knew these saved dimes would take them back to the wonderful places I had loved to see in those slide shows, presented by my grandpa.

In the evenings, I would often join him as he pored over maps deciding which new places they would visit on their next journey. He taught me to read maps during these times. Even more significantly, he taught me to dream about seeing other parts of our country and even the world. He taught me to read and study about a place before you traveled there. And, with Grandma, he taught me how to savor the memories once you returned.

In a way, this book started right there in my grandparents' living-room. They were the beloveds who opened my horizons to travel. They also taught me to be able to glean gems of pleasure and knowledge from all forms of travel. So often my grandpa would say, "It's important to see how the other half lives." Over the years, his simple saying became etched in my heart.

I'm forever grateful to them for this early training. Because of these experiences, this book has a shape and texture that it might not otherwise have. That shape and texture comes from the travel experiences that introduce each chapter: stories drawn from real travel encounters I've experienced on my spiritual path.

Just as my grandparents shared with me about their trips, I now want to show you how my life and, most importantly, my spiritual journey has been shaped by my travels, both far and wide.

Many of my travels grew out of my interest in history, as well as the impulse to see "just how the other half was living." They have always served to transport me back through time. I have been fascinated as to how humanity's rich tapestry has been intricately woven through and across the centuries.

To date, I've been to more than 40 countries and most of the fifty states. But the greatest trip of all, because it was my first, was when I was 17 and my grandparents took me with them to California.

We left Michigan on a cold early December morning. My grandpa always liked to get an early start and so on most mornings of the drive west so we were on the road by 5:00 am. We headed out of the driveway and finally connected to the now famous Route #66.

Along the way, we took time to stop at famous places like the "Petrified Forest" and also took several side roads so I could see some special sites. One of them was the "ghost town" of Jerome, Arizona, that my grandparents had discovered on one of their previous trips.

While in California, I got to visit Disneyland and Knotts Berry Farm. They also took me to an authentic Mexican restaurant where I had something I'd never heard of, let alone tasted--a taco. To this day, I still love to eat tacos. Then, on the night of December 31, my grandparents and their friends got me out of bed at 3:00 am. This early awakening was to take me to Pasadena in order to get a good spot from which to see the Rose Parade the next day. What a sight it was! The bands, the horses and, of course, the incredible flowered floats—all passing right in front of us. I was so blessed that my grandparents were willing to expose me to all these special activities.

Because I had to return for the start of school in January, I flew home by myself. I remember waking up the morning of my scheduled flight back to Michigan. I was so excited! It would be my first "big" plane ride. I had a new dress to wear and even had my hair done at a beauty salon! Of course, there were the many photos taken by my grandfather before I boarded the plane.

That trip to California was the first major trip of my life. My grandparents had done the best possible job of initiating me firsthand into the joys, challenges, and everyday blessings of venturing forth into the world. And, as this book will attest, it was truly only the beginning. All in all, this three-week trip expanded my life in ways that I have only now come to fully appreciate.

I now see that all of my trips have become like stepping stones to take me on what would be the most important journey of my life; the journey of self-realization that leads to what the mystics have termed the "eye of the heart." This is the inner journey. It's been taken by the saints, sages, and monks from every spiritual tradition. These holy ones led the way so that numerous unnamed ones could follow. Because of them, the inner journey beckons us today. Just as my grandparents had initiated me in the ways of seeing the world, there would come teachers into my life who would guide me in the ways of traveling the inner realms.

It's been said that we travel "without" to be able to go within. Nothing is ever wasted on any of these journeys. Everything in the outer world--every experience, encounter, circumstance, difficulty, and challenge—can be used to reveal who we are at the center-most part of our beingness. That is, if we develop the eyes to see and understand such things. In this way, every experience becomes an individually designed road map home to our essential self, this essential self then reveals the magnificence of the presence of God in our lives.

Along the way, I have found that what we are being taught or shown on this journey of self-exploration is often very simple. Sometimes it's about learning to accept or finding the courage to forgive. Sometimes it's trusting that our needs will be met. Sometimes it's about yielding or slowing down. And, most often, it's about learning how to love.

As my first spiritual teacher, the late Rev. Dr. Peggy Bassett, often said, "It's all God when you get to know it." To me, this means that every experience contains the seed of the Divine and the more we consciously engage our "seeing" on the journey, the more those seeds of experience are able to blossom into the moment-by-moment realization of the active presence of the Divine in our lives.

The world's great sacred scriptures are filled with promises from the Divine. I feel that one of our most important assignments as human beings is to connect with these promises and prove them right and true in our own lives. For me, during the times of difficulty which arise for all of us, I have found comfort in the scripture, "Lo, I am with you always, even unto the end of the world." (Matthew 28:20). I have touched this truth and experienced the fullness of its promise.

Part of my own spiritual preparation has been learning to accept the promises of God as real for me—as a gift for and to me. I had to journey through many places, both without and within, to believe and know that these great promises were really meant for me. Yes, for me.

Slowly though, these promises from the Holy Scriptures began to nurture and nourish the beginning foundation of my faith.

Actually, I think faith begins with hope. And even though in my own life, I couldn't always demonstrate what the scriptures promised, I did begin to hope for the kind of real faith that would bring the living revelation of such promises into my experience. So, in a real sense, this book is about the unfoldment of my faith.

Real enduring faith is the product of the best of both the Eastern and Western spiritual practices and approaches to life. Each of these traditions ask us to be able to take right action in the world but to do so demands that we know what is right for the highest good of all concerned, in any given circumstance. To be able to act in such a fashion is the beginning of true wisdom, and such wisdom unfolds through faith in and devotion to that which is greater than ourselves.

A friend once told me that on the spiritual path we often discover that we have been walking on the shoulder of the road instead of down its center. And there are even times when we get kicked off the shoulder and find ourselves in the ditch. This has certainly been true for me.

For example, within two days of taking my first trip out of the country, 1 found out how easy it is to get lost in new territory. It was just after my junior year in college and I had received a United States Department of Education Fellowship for a summer study in what was then known as Yugoslavia. I would be traveling with two professors from my university and 17 other students from other schools.

After the all-night flight out of New York, we arrived in Dubrovnik which is an ancient, beautiful city on the Adriatic Coast. While waiting for our connecting flight which would take us to the capital city, Belgrade, a few of us sat and had soft drinks at a little outside restaurant at this airport. There was a bright blue sky and the sun was glistening off the sea water as I listened to the "foreign" sounds that were being spoken around me. In that moment, I was simply overjoyed and filled with excitement by what lay ahead on this adventure into my first foreign country.

Upon arrival in Belgrade and after getting settled in my hotel room, I had time to take a walk before our formal welcoming dinner that evening. So, off I went down the city's grand Marshall Tito Boulevard. I wanted to get my "bearings," as my grandfather would say, and explore the area around the hotel. Not knowing how to speak or understand the Serbo-Croatian language, I decided I could find my way if I kept track of the names on the street signs. I selected one of the prominent signs and began to follow it. Before I knew it, I was further away from the hotel than I expected. Actually, I was now lost. It would take me a couple of frantic hours before I found my way back to our hotel. What had happened? I had been so careful about keeping track of the street signs. The answer came during our evening's dinner conversation. The street sign I had been following translated into "One Way!" Well, l never made that mistake again.

In this example, as well as others that will follow, you will see that I have landed and gotten lost in many a ditch, only to discover that what I needed to learn in preparation for something later down the road could have been learned and worked out only in that ditch.

This was not because of what existed in the ditch itself, but because of what being in the ditch called forth from within me. It was about what had to be strengthened and developed in me before I could proceed into deeper levels of self-realization.

We don't always know why we seem to veer off course on our journey. It's only later when we see the big picture that we recognize the true elegance of Spirit's guidance in our lives. For example, after teaching high school and college for ten years, I was drawn to the business world and worked in sales and marketing for another ten years. In both careers, I had a variety of experiences in many environments. Yet, I still felt unsettled; unsettled about how it all fit together and just what my "real" career would or could be. It was a very big question in my life at that time.

Then shortly after having moved back to Southern California in 1981, I connected with a graduate-school friend whom I hadn't seen in a few years. She invited me to go to church—a church with a woman minister. It seemed very strange to me to see a wonderful, elegant and powerful woman standing in the pulpit.

Sure enough, I went back to that church and, after several months, I felt the "calling" to the ministry. It was such a surprise! I then learned later, in ministerial training, that my previous careers in education and business had provided me with the much-needed knowledge and leadership skills to be able to successfully manage a large church organization. Spirit had designed the right ministerial training program for me long before I ever entered the actual work of the ministry!

What I have come to know is that living a spiritual life demands an inner pilgrimage and, like all great pilgrimages, it is to be traveled with care and reverence. I am convinced it is daily dedicated spiritual practice that keeps us consciously on the path and lifts us up when we end up in those darn ditches.

One important practice is the sacred pilgrimage. For Christians in the 10th and 11th centuries, there were three major pilgrimage routes—one to Jerusalem, one to Rome, and one to Santiago de Compostela in Spain. Today, these holy sites continue to call believers from around the world. The *Hajj*, is one of the five pillars of Islam, calling every devout Muslim to journey to the Holy *Kaaba* at Mecca in Saudi Arabia at least once in their lifetime. Hindu pilgrims have made their way to Varanasi, on the "Mother Ganges" river in India, for centuries. Followers of the Buddha in Thailand still journey to the Temple of the Emerald Buddha, the *Wat Phra Kaew*, in Bangkok. Similarly, devout Jewish believers travel to pray at the Western Wall in Jerusalem. Today, there are more tours to the world's sacred sites than could possibly be listed here.

Like these pilgrims, a major part of my spiritual evolution has occurred on these outer journeys. With each trip I took, something began to emerge in my understanding: I really was traveling *out* in order to go *within*. The experiences in the outer world served as a reflection of what was actually happening within the unfolding of my own soul's path to self-realization.

I have come to see that my inner journey had as many pitfalls, frustrations, delays, and difficulties as the outer pilgrimages. And, like the outer roads I've traveled, the inner journey revealed great joys, insights and understandings, as well as moments of incomprehensible peace.

In short, my journeys of evolution are very similar—one taking place in the outer world of form and the other being experienced in an invisible field of consciousness, accessed only through inner awareness.

Practice:

Contemplation is a very powerful way to be able to see where we come from and where we are. Where did your spiritual journey start? Who inspired you to see the Presence of God and supported you in finding your path?

Bless them and thank them for the service they provided in helping you to contact God. How has your path been made more fulfilling? Is your connection to Spirit stronger than it has ever been? Has your path opened doors to look deeply inside and connect with the Christ Presence? Know all is Divine Right Order as you contemplate these experiences.

Chapter 2: Boundaries

The Great Wall
Badaling, China

The temperature is way below zero and the wind chill factor makes it even colder on this January day. My fur hat and coat, coupled with the wool scarf tied around my face, make the freezing cold bearable, but icicles continue to form on my eyelashes.

Somehow, though, the cold doesn't matter, because I'm standing right where I've always known I would. I'm standing on one of the high watchtowers of the Great Wall of China, looking north across the mountains. I'm alone. There are no other tourists to steal away my attention.

Way beyond where my outer sight can take me is the expansive Gobi desert. From that northern land, the Manchu warriors began their move southward to conquer Imperial China and make it their own. As I look through the narrow opening in the fortifications of the watchtower, I imagine the hordes coming down on horseback from the distant Mongolian plains. I can almost hear them across the centuries... then, an all-too-familiar thought creeps into my awareness. How am I connected through time into humanity's long thread of history?

I pause and am overwhelmed by the power of the Wall. It's wide enough to take five men abreast on horseback or ten men marching side by side. Its length is a journey from Philadelphia to Las Vegas. It's about three stories high and is said to be the only man-made structure that the astronauts can see when orbiting the earth.

As I reflect upon these things, I conclude that it's the most enduring man-made boundary ever erected. Boundaries are built to keep others out and those we favor in. The Great Wall is an outer physical barrier but reminds me of my own inner walls that keep things safe until I'm ready to see them.

My experience at the Great Wall became an invitation for me to look where I haven't been willing to look before. I begin to wonder: What great wall within me was created as a defense to keep love out and darkness in?

In my late 20s I entered traditional analytic therapy to explore and resolve certain emotional conflicts that seemed to be blocking me from experiencing and expressing all that I wanted in my life. Thus, when I was fortunate to lead one of the first trade missions to the People's Republic of China after normalization of relations, it was a profound experience to stand on the Great Wall. On that Great Wall, I began to see the length to which a group of people would go to keep others out—people who looked, acted, and sounded different.

One of the valuable gifts of visiting China's Great Wall was that I came to learn that I had subconsciously developed my own intricate patterns of behavior that protected me from others and from situations that I thought could bring me harm. Therapy provided the avenue through which I learned to re-establish appropriate outer boundaries in order to become more functional in the world. Therapy also provided an opportunity for me to explore the depth of my own inner boundaries. It wasn't until years later, as the psychological work transformed into spiritual work, that I realized I would be called to transcend even those healthy inner boundaries so that my soul could be set free and be liberated in Spirit.

As I stood on the Wall that Sunday morning, I knew that so much of life, especially having healthy interpersonal relationships, was about boundaries. Like when and how to set them as well as trusting the decisions that evolved from having set them. In therapy, I learned to make the kinds of boundary choices that would be rewarded with success in the world. A portion of my therapy process also focused on being comfortable and at ease in setting outer boundaries while, at the same: time, moving through the process of disassembling and reorganizing dysfunctional inner ones.

I'm deeply grateful for the years (yes, years) I spent in therapy. It was in that room that I was able to develop and practice the skills that would make me a more self-aware and self-reflective person. I was lovingly supported by my therapist to "un-pack" old beliefs from which I had operated for most of my life, beliefs which had often taken me to places of doubt, frustration, sorrow, and even failure. I was also encouraged to examine my present-day experiences in light of those thoughts, beliefs, and patterns that had been born from my early childhood environment, and from the patterns that have come down through the generations from my ancestors.

When I began formal therapy in 1970, there weren't the choices that exist today. Back then, long-term individual therapy was a necessity if you were serious about answering the question, "Who am I?" In addition to private therapy, I also participated in some of the then newly emerging alternative modalities within the growing humanistic psychology arena but the bedrock of my process of healing and discovery was traditional, individual therapy.

I think therapy was the last half of the 20th Century's response to the ancient Greek philosopher Socrates, who said, "The unexamined life is not worth living."

I had thought about this statement many times since I had used it in high school to develop a talk for a district oratory competition. My speech teacher had devoted extensive time to coaching me on my presentation techniques. I was pleased with the talk that finally emerged, for I felt it integrated many of the things I had been thinking about and experiencing during that time in my young life. The talk addressed some of the great themes of the beginning of the 1960's, such as civil rights, the cold war and the emerging race to outer space.

As it happened, I placed second in the competition. Although disappointed, it was reassuring to me to see that my coach seemed surprised with my second-place position. He had thought that I would surely place first. Later that day, I was bewildered when he shared with me that one of the judges had privately told him that I would have gotten first place but that the fellow judges couldn't believe I had written the talk myself. I was stunned that they hadn't believed me! This incident set the stage for what I would later experience many times throughout my life: it was where I learned that in the world there is little support for the inner path or what Frost had first termed, "the road less traveled."

Back to the Great Wall. I believe there must have been an enormous impulse within the Imperial family and the Chinese warlords to build such a structure. Over time, I came to realize that it had been equally challenging to me to consciously and lovingly restructure the invisible patterns and boundaries within my very own being. It took such dedication and strength!

Where did this impulse to know myself originate? Upon reflection, it seems as if this yearning had always been a part of who I am.

Of course, little did I know that I was only at the beginning of my life-long search for self-knowledge. Years later, I would discover that the real work of my spiritual journey would demand that I cross over enormous boundaries of separation to behold that place of unitive realization in Spirit. Only in the awareness of Universal Oneness are all boundaries dissolved. ...But I'm getting ahead of myself.

I began the great search, or what the ancient cultural myths refer to as the hero's journey, much like others before me. I left the known world of my community, starting by being the first in my family to go to college and then, upon graduation, moving to the other side of the country.

Yes, I did make it back to California! As others like me, graduating in the latter part of the 1960s, I was filled with hope for a better world, and I wanted to be part of making it that way.

I arrived in Los Angeles on a bright and beautiful fall day.

Finding an apartment near the beach, I began to get ready for my first teaching position. It was to be at an overcrowded and basically rundown junior high school in the Watts area of Los Angeles. It was about a year after the "infamous" Watts riots and the rebuilding efforts had already begun. That's why I was there. I wanted to be part of something greater, or, as was commonly said at the time, I wanted to be part of the solution, not the problem.

I had brought my Midwestern work ethic, coupled with the great innocence of youth, with me to this challenging place. I stayed a year, which was longer than many of the teachers assigned to my school.

For several years after I left that job, I often told others that I had learned more than I had ever taught at that school. Most important, I learned that no matter where you find yourself, there's always a kindred soul who helps to show you the way.

In Watts, that person showed up as my supervising-department head. She had such love for the students as well as for her staff. Over and over again, she graciously transformed the difficulties of teaching in substandard conditions with overcrowded classes and armed guards on patrol. Even though this kind of situation is more typical of today, back then it was almost unheard of. And it was surprisingly different from what my own high school experience had-been in a new, large and beautiful suburban campus.

Looking back, I realize how many such "teachers" have been there for me. Many people reached out to guide and support me along the way. One of the greatest things about going beyond our own outer boundaries is discovering that there are always good and wonderful people on the other side. These beloved others are sometimes with us for a lengthy passage and sometimes simply join us for a short walk. Either way, they help us in finding our next steps.

I now see how the ability to connect with and trust these early teachers became the necessary practice which would eventually lead me to-connect with the real teacher—that great, sweet, small voice of intuition that I would come to know as my own inner divine guidance. Just as on the outside, I would have to traverse inner boundaries to make my way to that precious experience known as inner wholeness through communion with the Divine.

The outer journey, the traditional "hero's journey," leads us to self-actualization by way of reaching the outer limits of our human potential. The inner path then takes us to places beyond this time and life which are transcendent and eternal in nature. They are the domain of the Divine.

The history of humanity has shown that the Eastern or Oriental religions and cultures have emphasized the inner territory while the Western or Occidental ones have explored the outer territories by way of science and the scientific method. Although different, both approaches are valid. And both need to be utilized and integrated for humanity to reveal the wholeness of life that we are called to by the promises of all of the world's great religious traditions.

We are now approaching the time when it is no longer a choice of either one way or the other. Life is now calling us to use the best of both to come into a greater realization of who we really are. By this, I mean it's time for the highest of our humanness to be transformed into the promise of our greatest spiritual beingness.

After many of his healings Jesus would say, "Thy faith has made thee whole." I have spent hours contemplating this scriptural promise of God that came through

Jesus. I wanted to know if it was real. I wanted to know if it was really meant for me. I wanted to know how to have it.

Much to my astonishment, I came to see that Jesus didn't say, "God made you whole" nor did he say, "I made you whole." No, he said, "Your faith has made you whole." This meant that I had to take some form of action. I had to develop my faith. I had to bring something to this encounter with life. And finally, I had to take personal responsibility for the demonstration of wholeness. Yes, something *was* being asked of me in order for this promise from God to be made real in my experience of life.

Let us return to the idea of the "hero's journey." First of all, it demands that we go out and explore the world. And whether you go around the block or around the world, there is fruit to reap from a journey of any length or duration.

The result of our going out into the world is that we come to experience a "self" separate from family, traditions and old patterns of living. It's where we learn to master the world, if you will, and find our place in it. We become "individuated" beings. It's also where we meet these blessed others whom I have spoken about, and where we learn to face the many challenges of simply living in the world. Whether it is a difficult boss or a broken relationship, we are confronted with such challenges in order to develop courage. Yes, courage, for the development of courage is a major purpose of the "hero's journey."

In earlier times, courage meant bravery, but in today's world it has expanded to include the development of self-confidence through risk taking. Putting at risk our sense of self, who we think we are and how others see us, is the mental equivalent of what bravery was to earlier generations.

Let me give just one example. Today's risks, that is, risking our potential self-esteem, are what my ancestors' and my father's generation did on the battlefield of war.

He went beyond his boundaries, his known world, by joining the Navy. Much of what he was to become grew out of those early experiences during World War II. Likewise, my mother went beyond her known boundaries of family and traditions by entering the work force while my father was at war.

Of course, today we have men and women entering the military, but not in the great numbers of that past crisis. Also, it's a very different military life than it was in my father's generation.

The important point is that in every generation there is a movement that takes a person from his own world on a journey to a new one. He or she must be willing to pass through known boundaries in order to develop the kind of strength and courage that will later be needed for traversing the invisible inner boundaries of the soul to enter the spiritual life.

The journey out into the world is a journey of self-actualization. It is where a person's "self" gets developed and strengthened as he or she discovers who they are in the world. It's where a person finds out what they're made of through trial and error, success and failure. It's the process of gaining a sense of mastery in one's life. It is about our human potential and how functional and successful we experience ourselves to be.

Today, in our modern culture, this self-actualization is the main goal of a person's evolutionary journey. As we continue, we will find that it isn't the end of the process, but it is the necessary prerequisite for the inner journey that leads to self-realization. We need to have a functioning "self" to realize what a "self" is really made of.

In the same way, we have to be able to establish boundaries before we can transcend them. It is with the outer journey that we become self-actualized, while the fruit of the inner journey is self-realization. Self-actualization has to do with the outer path while self-realization is the work of the inner path. Self-actualization is essentially the product of the human personality whereas self-realization is the product of consciously knowing the soul's union with the Divine.

Self-realization begins with fully realizing that we are so much more than just our human personalities. The inner path of self-realization leads us to the highest level of our being which is Spirit.

It is only with the realization of an inner life that the soul can discover who it is for all eternity. It is only within the inner realms of awareness that the soul can go beyond the boundaries of personality, race, culture, and time to touch that which we were before birth and that which we will be after death. It's the only place where we can go beyond the pervasive boundary of time that makes our experience in this life seem so permanent.

There is more to realize about who we really are than what we can even imagine. And that's the great paradox. We never can truly imagine what it will be like living outside of or beyond the boundaries that currently give form to our lives. Oh, sure, we've seen pictures or heard of others' tales of such places. But we've never known it within our own skins, from the inside of our own eyes.

That's why we start the journey. Or, at least, that's why I did. I think there's something in many of us "seekers" that has wanted to be given birth, that has wanted to know more of what life is and how it works.

That's why I had to stand on the Great Wall of China. Sure, I had seen photos and I had heard stories, but no one, not one person, had prepared me for what it felt like on that cold January day. And truly, no one had ever indicated or even barely suggested what I would "see" about the nature of boundaries and the path of the soul. Much was revealed to me by standing there. As the wind whipped across my face, I saw the greatest of all manmade walls crawl its way through the mountainous terrain only to lose itself into the distant horizon.

Practice:

Boundaries are a way of surrounding us with a space of freedom to freely choose our path without limiting ideas or limited concepts. It's necessary to be able to say "no" to the world so that we can say "yes" to God. We do this by developing a healthy sense of self. You first have to have a self to later be able to transcend yourself. You don't lose your ego; instead, it must be made strong so you have the courage to surrender it into the light. Our individuality must get 'anchored' in Christ so we may live in freedom.

Chapter 3: Prayer

The Mountain Top
Pusan, South Korea

The bus has taken us as far as it can go up the winding hillside. The rest of the way we would have to walk. The nearly 200 clergy and leaders representing many faith traditions depart the bus and begin to form a snake-like procession up to the top ridge of the mountain. Slowly but surely, we make our way upward. I'm focused on watching where I place my feet, so I don't even notice the beautiful vistas of Southern Korea that surround me.

Finally, stopping to catching my breath, I find a spot to lean against a rocky ledge. It's here that I start to bring myself present to this place. Soon, the nervous talking of those around me stops and we begin to simply rest in the beauty of glorious surroundings on this clear, sunny day.

The inner serenity I am experiencing is soon broken by the group leader as he invites us into a form of prayer that I have never before experienced. He calls it "simultaneous out loud prayer" and begins to instruct us that after a few moments of silence, he would start and we could all join him by praying in our own way, with our own words, and in our own languages. He reminds us that there is power in group prayer and tells us we will truly enter into a blessed experience.

Then... the quiet. Resting in the silence, I take a deep breath and start to hear the beginning voices of the prayers. Soon, I gently raise my own voice to join with the others. The sounds become louder around me. They feel like clouds lifting my own prayer up to the heavens. Then, like rolling thunder, the voices begin to grow. The group prayer *seems to take on a life of its own as our many separate voices are transformed into one voice and one prayer. I can't tell where mine ends and the group's begins.*

I am lost, or perhaps I am finding myself, in the joined voices of our prayers. All too soon, the sounds trail off into a softness and sweetness I have never known. Finally, the silence returns and I know that experience of prayer has forever been changed.

As a child, I attended a nearby nondenominational Bible Church. My minister had been trained as a Southern Baptist and so it was quite fundamental in its teaching although, at the time, I didn't know exactly what that meant. I just remember loving the stories I was hearing in Sunday school as well as the lively, uplifting music I enjoyed during the church services.

There was also the "altar call" that took place at the end of each service. One Sunday morning I tentatively took the first step that led me down the long aisle of the sanctuary. It ended with me being on my knees before our minister. As he touched my head and prayed, I could feel God's love and peace. These feelings lasted only a few moments but they were indeed comforting to me. I understood that I was somehow being "saved" by this act of going to the altar. Now, I know those several walks I made up that aisle were my initial attempts to reach towards that invisible something called God.

It was in this church where I first learned to pray. These early prayers were being-spoken to a God "way up there." I wasn't sure where "there" was but I knew it was a very important place, and I certainly hoped I would get there someday. If I was a "good girl" and continued to pray and attend church, I might just make it!

In my early teens, I learned the "Lord's Prayer" as recorded in the scriptures (Matthew 6: 9-13). My Catholic friends used this prayer, but they also had many other prayers too. Actually, it seemed as if they had a prayer for just about everything—including a special prayer to the Virgin Mary. This prayer was done with beautiful beads called a rosary. Sometimes I would attend Sunday mass with them; I was in awe of the formality of their worship and the ornateness of their cathedral. My little church seemed so plain by comparison.

By the time I was in high school and fully active in social dubs and sports programs, I left church behind me. It's not as if I left God behind but I certainly left the church. Occasionally, I would find myself reaching out to God in prayer but this only happened when I was struggling with something: In other words, I just turned to God when I was hurting and needed help.

As an adult, it was the practice of prayer that took me back into my relationship with the Divine. It's where I began to talk about my life and my hopes and my dreams. I wanted to find out if God really existed for me. At first, like many others, I had some apprehension and fear. Questions such as, "Did I deserve to have a relationship with God?" and "Am I worthy of the blessings that such a relationship would bring?" filled by thoughts.

This was all put to rest when my Spiritual Director said, "Your willingness is your worthiness." There was power in that simple statement. It forced me to access my own willingness to acknowledge this relationship. It also asked me to explore whether I was willing to learn to really love and be of service to others.

Over the years, I have come back to this place, asking these same questions about my worthiness. Humbly, my answer has always been "yes." I have realized that my willingness to enter into this relationship was essential for me to progress on the spiritual journey. I think my spiritual work has always been, first and foremost, about my own willingness. And each time this issue was settled within me, I felt a great sense of worthiness flow through me.

Then, in one way or another, a greater good would always be revealed.

Many people come back to the act of prayer' because there is no other place for them to go. Perhaps they have exhausted all other worldly avenues for healing or comfort. Still others turn to prayer out of having been "broken open" due to some challenge or life difficulty. However, there are those few fortunate ones who come to a prayer life out of a yearning to simply know more of who they are and how they fit into the great scheme of life.

I've also discovered that our prayer life changes as our relationship with God grows and deepens. Many people speak their first prayers as adults out of need or desperation. These kinds of prayers are most reflected in the idea of beseeching God to save us. In our suffering, we want to blame someone or something for our problems and then want God to save us from the torment we feel those others have caused us. It feels as if we are doomed and that the world is against us. At such times, we are lost and seek to be found. We have no other place to go and so God becomes our last hope. In a beseeching prayer, we may shout out a cry for help or meekly whisper it as if we were saying our last words.

During such times, some people may recall a prayer from their childhood. This was the case of a man I once knew. He was a recovering alcoholic who told me that his alcoholism had ruined his career and was about to destroy his family. He was, as is often said, at the end of his rope, which means he was hanging on to life by what seemed a thread. He had "hit bottom" as it is known in Alcoholic Anonymous.

He told me that after a particularly difficult drinking binge, he was lying alone in the bed of a run-down hotel. He was desperate and ready to reach out, but to what, he wasn't sure. The only prayer he remembered from childhood was the Lord's Prayer. He said it aloud and he kept saying it aloud over and over again. That prayer literally lifted him up and took him into the healing rooms of AA.

He never drank again. The very act of reaching out to something greater than himself had saved him and he was redeemed and began to live his life from what that act of prayer had meant.

Other people have misconceptions about prayer or resist it all together. For example, one of my ministerial friends shared with me the experience of counseling with a member of his congregation who was in the midst of pain. This person was "beside herself" and didn't know what to do. The minister listened to her problems, which were numerous, and at the end of the conversation suggested they pray together. A look of surprise flashed across the woman's face and she responded by saying, "Oh no, I can't pray! Prayer is for when you're really in trouble!!!"

Today, I know that prayer has been the activity through which I began to have the eyes to see and the ears to hear the invisible side of life. But it took many years. In the beginning of my adult journey back to God, it felt as if the Divine was still outside of me in some universal domain way beyond my reach. As I continued in my prayer practice, I began to sense a change. Gradually, I entered the "space" of having the heart to feel the indwelling Presence of the Holy One.

Prayer is often the first step that we take to enter into a conscious relationship with the presence of God. In the Western religious traditions, the spoken prayer has been the bedrock for our relationship with the Divine. However, the common practice of using mantras in the Eastern traditions serves somewhat the same purpose. It's described a little differently but the intent is the same; i.e., it's using speech, both silent and vocal, to turn away from the outer world, settle our minds, and give full attention to the sacred mystery that is beyond us.

It seems to me that the presence of the Divine is always there, standing watch and waiting for us to call upon it; waiting for us to initiate the relationship, just as millions of others have done before us. Each prayer we pray becomes a building block to a deeper communion and fuller realization of our union with the Divine. In this way, prayer builds faith.

It's important to remember that prayer is not some rule we have to follow to please God. Instead, it's one of many spiritual practices that take us more deeply into our relationship with the Divine. Every time we begin a prayer, we are first and foremost acknowledging there is a relationship. In prayer, we speak into this relationship.

One time when I was the guest minister at a church in Florida, a woman became upset when I said, "Most people have a closer relationship with their problems then they do with God." Well, she didn't like this and she told me so. Perhaps she didn't like what she saw about her own problems. Anyhow, she began to calm down when I explained that this is the likely outcome when we spend more time in relationship with our problems—thinking about them, talking about them, worrying about them—than we do in fostering a relationship with God. In other words, we give more attention and time to our problems than we do to engaging in activities that will enhance and support us in experiencing a "closer walk" with the Divine.

Actually, the path of spiritual practice requires that we learn to turn away from our problems and begin to spend time developing our relationship with the Divine. To be able to do this, we must first recognize the presence of God, then realize it as our own divine nature, and finally reveal this nature into expression through us and into the world.

These three "R's," recognition, realization, and revelation, represent the dynamic pattern or template for the embodiment of all higher truths. With recognition, we gain knowledge and with realization, that knowledge is integrated into who we are as the light of wisdom. Finally, revelation is about "walking our talk" and putting into action that which we have now embodied as truth. However, it sounds a lot easier than it actually is.

Most everyone has experienced having a good idea and not being able to make it happen. We all have had wonderful thoughts and dreams that never manifested. It's easy for our minds to "talk the talk" and for our thoughts to follow along. However, it's much more difficult to get our bodies in motion as evidenced by anyone who has ever started an exercise program. This reality is what Jesus was referring to when he said "... the spirit indeed is ready, but the body is weak." (Matthew 26: 41).

Another way of approaching our relationship with God is to see the Divine as the ultimate Principle of Good in the Universe. The late 19th century the American mystic, Emma Curtis Hopkins, often said that "God is the Good we can all agree upon." This "good" is what is pointed to by such enduring ideals as joy, peace, wholeness, love and abundance. In fact, these are all qualities that we attribute to the Divine.

Prayer becomes the main practice by which we develop a greater awareness of these attributes and the means by which we come to know, at least in part, this "all-good." Through a dedicated prayer life, the all-good that is God then begins to move through our thoughts and into our lives.

Out of our devotion to and acknowledged relationship with the Divine, this good now recognized can be realized within us and then revealed through us. In this way, we become open, individual expressions of the Universal Life that is God. We activate, nurture and honor this relationship every time we enter into prayer.

Simply put, prayer is when we speak to God. But, at its highest level, it becomes the voice of Spirit speaking through us and speaking God's good into our lives. At this level of understanding we become the center through which the all-good of God can be realized in the world. How are we to come to know this all-good? Let me begin by first asking, "Do you believe there's good for you?"

Stop and pause for a moment to consider this question: Do you really believe there's good for you in your life?

If your answer is yes, that's the first step. In fact, this idea can be turned into a simple prayer, as:

"There is good for me and I believe I ought to have it. This good is what God promised the world through the Holy Scriptures. I accept it for myself here and right now.

I also claim and accept it for all humanity. I now proclaim that God knows how to reveal this good into my experience of life. I am open to God's guidance for my good and am grateful for God's graciousness in my life. Amen."

If you don't already have a prayer practice, I would invite you to read this little prayer aloud and keep reading it aloud on a daily basis until you see your own good beginning to be demonstrated.

This is what it means to practice, and prayer is a practice. It is the practice of first turning within so that the words of our prayers arise from that which is highest in us. In this way, every prayer we speak is a blessing to our souls.

Prayer changes us because of what takes place in our hearts and minds by the very act of praying. Ultimately, prayer is about transforming us from the inside out. Just as it was said by St. Paul in the scriptures,

Do not conform to the pattern of this world, but be transformed by the renewing of your mind. Then you will be able to test and approve what God's will is—his good, pleasing and perfect will. [Romans 12: 2}

When we pray from this understanding, we are literally acknowledging that there is something greater to which we are connected.

Jesus called this great inner reality the "Father within"—the "Father" being the principle of life itself. This principle is pointing to an inner experience that, ultimately, is beyond any words we may have for it. It is simply the activity of the life that is God individualized in us, as us, and for us, ever expressing through the unfoldment of the seed of Light that has been in our souls from the beginning. When Jesus said to pray in his name (John 15: 16), I have interpreted that to mean for me to pray "inside" his name, or to pray from the consciousness that so filled him[1]. That is, from the light and love that is the consciousness of Christ.

---

[1] The Hebrew word *shem* means "nature, quality, essence" and so

I believe there is, and has always been, a part of us that wants to answer the call and surrender into the mystery of having a relationship with the Divine.

It's not easy to take the first step. It's not easy to say our first prayer. It's not easy to trust that which is invisible. It's not easy to "let go and let God." It's not easy to turn away from the world and face ourselves. It's not easy to reach into the invisible side of life. Yet all, not just some, spiritual practice requires that we repeat these acts of surrender to the Divine over and over again. Prayer is just one of the first places where we learn to practice this "letting go" and come face to face with what it means to us. However, the more that we do it, the more abundant are our blessings.

Prayer is most effective when practiced on a daily basis, rather than waiting until being confronted by some drastic challenge or difficulty. This is why prayer must eventually become the foundation for our daily, dedicated spiritual practice. In short, prayer is just one of the ways we meet our own divine nature so that we can live our lives from the highest truth of our being. Of course, the issues of the day try to pull us down from this exalted place that we experience in prayer. The pressures and demands of daily living seem to steal us away from the inner sacred sanctuary that a prayer life creates.

We will be pulled out into the world. Yet, when we return to prayer, to go within and nurture our relationship with the Divine, we will be made new again... and again... and yet again.

And, oh, the blessings of being in sweet communion with the Divine! From the first awareness of inner communion in prayer, we recognize that we now have a place, an inner altar, to return home to.

Another change or passage then takes place during our prayer life. It begins to happen when we've had a strong prayer practice but the comfort that we previously experienced from it doesn't seem to be there anymore.

"in my name" invites us to enter that nature, that quality, that essence.

It's as if there isn't any "juice" in our words. We pray and yet still feel empty. Or our prayers aren't bringing forth the demonstrations we had enjoyed in the past. It may also become harder and harder to find the right words, let alone speak them.

Sometimes we may even stop praying altogether.

This is actually an important place to be. Let me explain. It signals that we are at one of what will be many "Holy Jumping-Off Places" on our journey. It means we are being given the opportunity to enter into a deeper prayer practice. It means that we must engage other practices to activate a deeper level of inspiration from within our souls. It means we have to face the struggle of once more standing in faith. It means we have to enter into a new level of devotion. It means that what had previously been given with little effort on our part now must be consciously worked for. It means we must learn to "...walk by faith and not by sight" (2 Corinthians 5: 7)

That sounds pretty harsh but it is the necessary preparation for us to become initiates on the path of self-realization. It means we have to take responsibility and action for our spiritual evolution. We must begin to more consciously *initiate* our relationship with the Divine. In other words, we must really want it.

There are times on the path when we begin to take this precious relationship that opens up within our prayer life for granted. It's almost as if we are being brought to our knees again. And I've certainly been on my knees in this place more than once.

As I said in the beginning, we often turn to God through prayer because of some drastic life difficulty. Now, at this stage, the world seems to be going along "okay" but something appears to be missing from the one place that has been most sacred to us. Again, there's an emptiness that overtakes us. So, what are we to do?

Unfortunately, this is where some people stop practicing. It's as if they're saying "See, I knew it would never really work, anyway." Actually, it *is* working, because we are being brought to this stage to be strengthened in our prayer life, in our relationship with the Divine. It's absolutely NOT the time to turn away. Now, more than ever, we must engage in the practices that will take us into the next stage of spiritual realization.

The activities that will get us back on track in our prayer life are the kinds of activities that lift our spirits and renew our hope in life. Some of these include listening to inspiring music, reading motivational books, talking to a friend and confessing our fears, attending a new class, or seeing a movie or video. The very best one of all for me has been to read scripture or other writings of sacred truth aloud. This is because there is what is called a "transmission" of spirit, of love, in the writings of truth. The scriptures refer to this transmission as an anointing.

By speaking words of truth aloud, we are both reading and hearing them. And our souls love to experience the sweet elixir that the radiant words of truth convey. By reading aloud, we are actually touching truth the only real place that we can, that is with our tongues. The scriptures tell us that death and life are in the power of the tongue. (Proverbs 18: 21) Thus, what we speak matters. We also learn that words of truth are powerful and creative. We learn that our words can be life-giving or life-denying. Spoken words of truth have the potency to lift us up from discouragement, suffering, and even sickness.

Over the years of my prayer life, I have certainly cycled through this passage of discouragement and feeling "off course" many times. Just so you know, and I'm sorry to have to say it, but it's not a one-time thing. However, each passage through it deepened my faith, strengthened my practice, and lifted my spirit. I have seen it happen for hundreds of other people too. And I know it can for those of you who are reading these very words. You might say that I've learned to "wait upon the Lord" as the scripture says. (Isaiah 40: 31)

However, I know of many instances where I learned that what I had been praying for wasn't appropriate or right for me as my life began to unfold. As I said, prayer changes us and so the very act of praying changed something in me. Thus, the "new" me no longer needed those previous things I had been affirming in my prayers. It's a paradox. Yet, I now know that it's part of the preparation that taught me to quit asking for things, whether it was the things of the world that I wanted to acquire or experiences I wanted to enjoy.

For example, when I was first beginning to have an active prayer life, I would write out my prayers in a big sketchbook, like artists use. One day, as I was looking back over the book, it occurred to me that most of the prayers were lists of things I wanted from God. It's as if I had put all my goals up to that time in my life in a basket and said, "Here, God, do whatever you do and make these happen for me." It's as if I was treating God as some kind of "cosmic bellboy." Granted, some of my prayers were answered but many on my lists were not. It was an "ah ha" moment. I saw how I had been going to God to get what I wanted. Now, I began to realize that I needed to ask what God wanted from me.

As this question started to move through my prayer life, I knew that I had to be willing to seek a greater awareness of God through wrestling with my own doubts and fears. I came to understand that this precious relationship with the Divine was the gift, the very answer to all my prayers. And if there was never another demonstration of it in my life, the relationship, in itself, would be enough. Slowly, I began to go to God with not only a more open heart but also with open hands. In other words, I began to come with my hands raised in praise instead of having them out in front of me trying to grab for the kinds of things I had written on my prayer lists.

This shift in me is what actually led me into the next phase of my prayer life, the phase of true inner realization of my own divine nature as a beloved of God. Sometimes, this prayer experience is called God-communion or the mystical marriage in Christ. It's that to which all the mystics, sages, and saints have pointed. It's when what we are praying "to" is where we are praying "from."

I have also received great value out of praying for others as well as having others pray for me. In fact, I've been praying weekly with one prayer partner or another for over twenty-five years. My faith has been expanded through the power of agreement that is realized when two or more people pray together. I have come to believe that the power of agreement that is experienced through group prayer is one of the most important teachings of mystical Christianity. It's what Jesus taught his disciples when he said,

Again, I tell you that if two of you on earth agree about anything you ask for; it will be done for you by my Father in heaven. For where two or three come together in my name, there am I with them. (Matthew 18: 19 & 20)

I've also had the opportunity to guide hundreds of people in their prayer life. This has taken place in classes I've taught, in workshops and retreats I've facilitated or with individuals for whom I have served as a Spiritual Director. I have seen people's relationships, financial matters, career challenges, and health situations healed and transformed through their willingness to engage in the practice of prayer. Each, in their own way, found the courage to do what was asked of them and as they continued in the practice of prayer, their communion with the Divine was strengthened.

As a result, God's promises became real for them in their experience of life. In fact, in every case, each of them was delivered from difficulties and old ways of living. Each of them was raised up into new life through their faith, the kind of faith that's established through a dedicated daily prayer practice.

So it is with us today. God's promises call to us. If we respond by entering into our relationship with the Divine through prayer communion, we are changed. Again, prayer transforms us. And, in turn, our experience of the world is also changed and changed for the better. What becomes important on this path of prayer is the deepening of where we are praying from.

When prayer becomes personal, so, too, our relationship with God becomes personal. The only God we can ever know is the God of our own understanding. Prayer is the sure method and practice that expands our understanding and deepens our personal knowingness of the Divine.

As you continue to read further on in this book, you will find that I've benefited from exploring many different religious traditions, but I'm not a follower of these traditions. For example, I studied Islamic mysticism (Sufism, as it is called in the West} in Turkey, practiced with Buddhist monks, and taught from the *Bhagavad-Gita* of Hinduism. There was great value for me in my experiences within each of these traditions, for they always served to expand my own personal understanding and relationship with the Divine.

In a sense, each of these "side paths" led me back to where I had started. And where I had started was with the teachings of Jesus, with those stories I had learned and loved as a child. I can now see the fullness and richness of where I have been led on my path. I can also reflect upon the times that I had been lost but was humbled in finding myself... again... and again. Just like I had experienced on that mountain top in South Korea.

Practice:

Prayer transforms us. Simply put, prayer is when we speak to God. What becomes important on the path of prayer is the deepening of where we are praying from. At the highest level it becomes the Voice of Spirit speaking thru us and speaking God's Good into our lives.

There are many forms of prayer. Whatever practice you use make sure it aimed at connecting with the Pres-

ence. It is important to not ask for specific things or personal desires. Prayer is to connect with God and get out of the way so Spirit can demonstrate the Divine Right Order in any situations in our life. (Some examples may be found at the back of this book.)

Chapter 4: Meditation

The Convent

Albuquerque, New Mexico

It's the middle of the fifth night of a ten-day silent Vipassana meditation retreat led by a Buddhist monk... in a Catholic convent. I'm in one of the cells that housed various nuns on their pilgrimages to God. I wonder how many images of the Divine this room has seen and how many prayers of desperation and longing as well as thanksgiving and gratitude have these walls witnessed? I'm probably just one person in a long line of other seekers who has come to this place for solace.

It's extremely quiet: there are absolutely no sounds from outside these four walls. Things are very different for me now that I've spent five days of silent looking into my "self." Five days of watching my thoughts. Five days of sitting and seeing into my mind. Five days that at times crept like years and at others sped by in a single breath. Lying here at night, it's hard to tell the difference between waking and sleeping.

And there are the dreams. They have become an avenue of freedom for long suppressed feelings and images from my subconscious mind. I have experienced what has been termed "lucid dreaming," as if I'm consciously orchestrating my own dreams.

But now, something new shows itself to me in the middle of my night. I'm awake. I open my eyes and the room is black nothingness but when I close my eyes all I see is sparkling light Opening my eyes again, the darkness falls upon me. Closing my eyes once more, I'm bathed in the dancing light that seems to fill my being. I breathe and surrender into the light as I am embraced in its sweet elixir of love. What is this peace-filled inner light that is greater than any darkness and purer than any sun?

If prayer is the practice in which we learn to "talk" With God, then meditation is the practice we engage in to "listen" to God. All religious practices support us in working out our own relationship with the Divine. On the Eastern path, the listening aspect of this relationship is called meditation. In the Western traditions, it's been known as entering the silence, contemplation, centering, or simply worshipping in the quiet.

As we engage in the practice of meditation, we are actually giving our attention to our relationship with the Divine. And, as with all healthy relationships, there are times when we speak and times when we listen. It's how we get to know one another. It's also how we continue to grow together in friendship, kindness, respect, and love—whether it be with our family members, friends, or professional colleagues. It's no different in regard to our relationship with God.

We must continually enter into practices that support the deepening in love of this sacred relationship with the Divine.

I had known about the importance of meditation for years before I actually tried it myself. It was simply one of those things a person was supposed to do on the spiritual journey. I certainly had plenty of friends and colleagues who encouraged me to begin.

However, it seemed I was never able to slow down enough to learn how to do it.

I had experienced guided visualizations and meditations in church classes and other kinds of workshops. It was easy and enjoyable to participate in these group experiences but I found it was much more difficult to know what to do when I was alone. The big question continued to loom before me, "How was I to begin?"

Eventually, I borrowed a set of "How To" meditation tapes from a friend. I think they must have been on my bookcase for several days, if not weeks, before I finally picked a day to start listening to them. I decided my "place" for meditation would be the comfortable chair I had in my bedroom overlooking the Pacific Ocean in Del Mar, California. I sat down and put on the headphones and began to follow a variety of instructions that had to do with relaxing various parts of my body. I was also guided in becoming aware of my breathing. This experience seemed pleasant enough but I still didn't feel like I was "getting" it. After a few days of listening to the same tape, I was ready to give up or, at least, find another way to do it.

Next, someone told me to begin by setting a kitchen timer for five minutes and just sit down, relax and "watch" my breathing. Surely, I could sit still and do this for five minutes!

Again, I picked the morning I would try this approach and set my timer for five minutes. Well, I thought I would just die! I must have looked at the timer about twenty times in the first couple of minutes alone.

Everything in me just wanted to get up and run from that chair.

However, a part of me was willing to keep at it, if only for a few days. Soon, I began to notice that when I sat down, my "mind" would go crazy. First, I would think about everything that I had to get done that day. Next, I would move into wonderful fantasies about something I wanted to have happen in the future. Yes, I know I was supposed to bring my awareness back to my breathing when these things took place but I first had to become aware that I had "gone away" before I could choose to "come back." I still didn't really "get" it but, at least, I could now sit there for the full five minutes and only look at the timer a few times.

During this period when I was struggling to begin my meditation practice, I subscribed to the *Quartus Report*, a newsletter written by author John Randolph Price and his wife Jan.

Such books by him as *Practical Spirituality* had been helpful and instructive to me in the beginning of my spiritual work. One day the newsletter arrived and, sure enough, there was a short article by Jan about how to begin meditating. She made it sound so simple.

The article let me know that I didn't need a strange or unusual mantra; nor did I need any fancy clothes, cushions, or bells. What I did need to do was to simply sit down and attempt to be at rest. Then I was to close my eyes and bring my inner awareness to the circular pattern of my breathing. As I was inhaling, I was to silently say, "I am." Then, as I was exhaling, I was to add a quality of God that I wanted to identify with for that day, such as love, joy, peace or beauty. It not only made sense to me but it "clicked" when I tried it.

That was more than twenty years ago and I'm still meditating as part of my daily spiritual practice. Even today, there are times when I return to those simple ideas offered by Jan Price.

A good variation on her original instructions came to me from noted futurist Barbara Marx Hubbard. Again, on the inhale, say silently, "I am" and on the exhale say, "Here Now." I have found this to be especially useful when my thoughts are "running wild." It's been a proven way for me to bring my attention back to the pattern of my breath and to return my awareness to the eternal moment of now.

Speaking about the "moment," all methods of meditation practice prepare us to live in and from the "now" moment. Usually. people are either living out of their pasts or fleeing into some imagined future fantasy life. Things like regret, unfinished anger with others, disappointments and bitterness keep our thoughts tied to things, people and events from our past while things like our hopes, dreams, wishes, and fantasies keep us focused on the future.

We can neither live in the past nor in the future, for the past has already taken place and the future has yet to come. The only time it may *appear* that we are living in our past or in the future is within our minds. And living in our minds in either of these places keeps us from living our lives in the only place we truly can, that being the present moment.

You've possibly heard the story about the woman who talked with her close friend after she had a date with a man she had been admiring. By the end of the conversation, her friend had to finally say, "Stop, it's too early for you to pick out the china!" You see, the woman had already fled into her future fantasy of getting married. And you can be sure that the man hadn't decided whether or not he even wanted to go on a second date. Of course, this is a funny little example but it underscores the point I'm making.

With the guidance of my Spiritual Director, I began to explore my past. I soon discovered what being part of the first wave of women to enter into the professional work force in the late sixties had meant to me. I saw how important it was for me to set a good example; i.e., work hard for my success in order to pave the way for those women who would follow me. The common advice during those years was that for a woman to get ahead she would have to work twice as hard as her male colleagues. I had sure taken that so-called "advice" to heart!

Going even deeper, I found out how important it was to me to "prove something" to my father. To prove I could do it. To prove I could be a success. To prove I could accomplish my goals. All along, my inner voice was saying, "No matter what it takes, keep struggling and work hard." Somehow, in my own belief system, I had "work" and "struggle" wired up together. It's as if they meant the same thing.

And this cluster of a belief became "married" to other beliefs I held about money. The resulting pattern of behavior meant that when money was involved, I would have to struggle and work hard for everything I earned.

Actually, there came a time when I had to face the fact that I'd been just like that woman in the story. I had used my fantasies of some future good to mask the fears and doubts that were buried within me. For example, I had thought my life would really be good after I graduated from college, or when I got a better job, or when I got married. The problem I had to face was that after "getting" each of these, I found myself wanting another degree, a different job and yes, even a new husband!

Yet, here I was, loving my work as a minister. I certainly didn't want to jeopardize either my career or my health and well-being by continuing to live out of this cluster of false beliefs. I wanted to be set free of the beliefs that chained me to patterns of the behaviors that I now was beginning to discover. Through the wise counsel of my Spiritual Director, I begin to sense that I didn't have to behave in these ways. I began to have the eyes to see that there were other ministers who were living prosperous lives filled with grace and ease. I also saw many of the members of my own congregation living in a greater freedom than what my beliefs had allowed for me.

It was in meditation that I could finally witness these "error" thoughts as the "illusions" of my mind and not the truth of my being. The more I looked into them, the more I saw the impact they had on my entire life. 1 saw how 1 had placed work before my spiritual practice, my relationships and even my health.

Because I was willing to continue with my practice of meditation, I was given the "light" to see such false beliefs and attitudes that had lived in the dark recesses of my subconscious mind.

In this experience, it's easy to see how the light of inner awareness enables us to explore and witness how our own beliefs shape and direct our experience of life. Meditation is where we practice expanding the light of our awareness.

As I continued my practice, I began to realize how my issues from the past caused me to flee into these future fantasies. In much the same way, there were many times when I also found myself living in fear of the future. In fear that I wouldn't get what I wanted or needed. I also had doubts that there wouldn't be enough money, success or even love. In other words, there were times when I feared that my dreams would never become a reality.

All of these kinds of thoughts are simply the "noise" that incessantly fills our minds and keeps us from experiencing fully any one given moment in our lives. Actually, it's as if our minds are made up of a swarm of thoughts, beliefs and attitudes that stem from such fears. Some of these we may recognize but many are so habitual that we don't even know we have them. That is, until we sit down to meditate and begin to see how much swarming is really taking place just below the level of our conscious awareness.

Most of these swarming thoughts are born out of past experiences of pain and suffering. In turn, they end up as deeply held opinions that we assume to be true. And these opinions may or may not be based on factual information, let alone higher spiritual truths and ideals. Because these thoughts and opinions have been suppressed within our minds, we rarely have access to them unless we spend time in therapy or enter into a regular program of spiritual practice.

Like most everyone, there have been many days when I skipped my meditation practice. This was especially true in the early years.

As a matter of fact, it took at least five years for my practice to be really anchored into my daily routine. There have also been times when it became what I call "shaky" or "ragged." By this I mean that I would try to do it quickly or I would use it as a way to plan my day.

Sometimes I even used it to imagine what I was going to say to someone who had upset me. But, through all the ups and downs, I always came back to the chair, just not the same chair I started with.

Thinking about this, it occurs to me that my chairs changed as I went through the successive stages of deepening in my practice.

There was even a period in my life when I got in the habit of meditating and praying while "sitting up" in my bed. This started when I was doing a lot of traveling and staying in hotels and other people's homes. My Spiritual Director had to remind me that it wasn't a good idea to do my spiritual practice in bed, for my bed was a place to *sleep* while the purpose of spiritual practice was to *wake* me up! Obviously, I went back to using a chair.

I've also experienced falling asleep while in meditation. There have been times when I just couldn't stay awake, especially when I was meditating alone. I've seen it happen in groups too. Every once in a while, someone in a group meditation will begin to snore. At such times, it's usually the person sitting next to them that gently wakes them up. I've experienced being on both sides of this.

I'm sure, as you continue in your practice, you'll find it's easier to spend more time doing it. This is because of the many benefits that will become apparent to you. For example, the more you are able to still your mind, the less reaction you will have when things in the world don't go the way you expected or wanted them to. The time that you have spent in meditation will teach you to "pause" in the midst of the circumstances and difficulties of your life. During this "pause" period, you will be able to make better choices about what is right for you in any given moment. In this way, you'll begin to have a greater sense of mastery over your life.

I really saw this when I was attending a series of weekend meditation retreats in Los Angeles. One of these was led by a Zen monk from the Japanese Buddhist tradition. When he walked into the room the first day, he was carrying a big, long, intricately carved walking stick.

Our small group was jerked out of the quiet when he began banging it on the wooden floor. Only it didn't stop there. Each time he saw someone nodding off, a huge bang would resound through the room. Also, he somehow knew when one of us was going "away" from the task at hand that is to stay "awake" within. Again, there would be a bang on the floor. This man was a real "drill sergeant" compared to the other monks I'd trained with, but his lesson has stayed with me.

Over the centuries, meditation has provided one of the main avenues for "seeing" or "witnessing" the content of our own minds. It is important to be able to "see" our thoughts because, until we do, we will never be able to change them. This is because seeing that what we've been believing is *not true* can actually begin to change our lives.

Thus the practice of meditation is not a short-term venture, for its benefits are only accrued through continued and regular practice over extended periods of time, throughout one's life.

I don't think it really matters whether you choose an approach from the Eastern or the Western traditions to begin meditating. The important thing is to find a method that works for you and then continue to do it. Yes, just do it! It will make all the difference in your experience of life as well as in your own spiritual growth and unfoldment.

Practice:

If prayer is the practice in which we learn to "talk" With God, then meditation is the practice we engage in to "listen" to God, Source, Christ, or other names.

There are many forms of meditation. One of the easiest is to find a quiet location where you won't be disturbed then relax your body and sit quietly. Focus on your breath, feel the cool air going in and the warm air going out. If your mind wanders come back to your breath.

As your mind quiets, listen; what do you hear? Ask for clarity; peace and understanding will take place. Be open to receiving peace and understanding. You can do this simple meditation anywhere or anytime.

Seek and you will find your own form of meditation.

Chapter 5: Belief

The Concorde
Over the Atlantic Ocean

Elegantly dressed, I'm sitting in the luxurious gray leather seat. It is the place where I had wanted to be since I first learned of the joint development of the supersonic jet transport plane by British Airways and Air France. The Concorde... I had seen it over the years when, on other planes, I passed near it on the tarmac at Dulles and at Dallas-Fort Worth airports. It was always exciting to observe its movable front beak and sleek lines. It reminds me of my favorite bird, the seagull. Now, here I am, sitting in my very own seat on this magnificent aircraft!

We have just lifted off from Kennedy Airport in New York on our way to London's Heathrow. As we reach cruising altitude, the digital display on the bulkhead reports our air speed as well as both the outside and inside temperatures. I notice the numbers showing our air speed increasing dramatically while the outside temperature is rapidly decreasing. Soon, we will pass through the invisible barrier of Mach 1 which Chuck Yeager had first pushed through over the California desert on October 14, 1947, in a Bell X-1 research plane. We will be flying faster than the speed of sound.

I touch the window and feel the heat of the resistance produced as this aluminum and steel bird slices through the air. Suddenly, my whole body is pressed back into the cushioned seat. This gentle jolt is the physical confirmation of the digital index. We have passed through Mach 1.

I can't hear our sonic boom for by now it is already miles behind us. We are traveling faster than our own sound!

Looking out the window, I notice the slight curvature of the earth, and for the first time with my own eyes, I see that our world isn't flat.

I had followed the development of the Concorde from its beginning, and longed for the time I, too, would be able to fly on it.

In a few years that time was a reality. One of my minister friends joined me for the journey. We flew into New York and found our way to where the Concord had its own terminal. We arrived early as instructed and saw that the nose of the Concorde was lowered, and it came right up to the window.

We settled in the lounge and joined the others who were waiting to board. We were served wonderful food as we met our flying companions. It seemed as if the excitement was expanded as we met the wonderful people who would share our journey with us.

We entered the plane and found our seats. The stewards continued to bring us beautiful gifts. Of course, the Champagne was flowing as the joy was for all of us who had dreamed of flying on the Concorde.

Finally, the time came for us to board the plane. (2 seats on each side). It was smaller than I had thought but as I sat down in the luxurious gray leather seat, I was elated!

The pilot's voice came over the sound system when we went out over the Atlantic to go through Mach 1.

As we entered London's Heathrow Airport there were people lined up to welcome the Concorde back to London. We then took a taxi to the home of a friend we were going to stay with for a week before we would take the QE2 ship back home to New York Harbor. Little did I know that the return to the USA would include hundreds of people lined up to welcome us back.

Even today, the memory of that extraordinary journey fills my heart with joy.

Practice:

This is a simple prayer treatment that is very effective. Whatever the condition, here is a way to make it a denial-and-affirmation prayer. Say the following:
- *I don't believe in the condition; I believe in the demonstration.*
- *I don't believe in loss; I believe in The Christ.*

Repeating these phrases will keep you from focusing on the problem.

You can apply it in various scenarios:
- *I don't believe in disorder, confusion, bad luck (or various other states or conditions);*
- *I believe in Spirit, Jesus Christ, God, The Presence (or any aspect or name of the divine power that you use).*

Repeating these simple phrases helps the mind to stop over-thinking the problem or condition so a demonstration can happen.

I have seen many demonstrations of lost items being found or circumstances changing without any more effort than turning it over to Spirit.

Chapter 6: Surrender

The Mosque
Istanbul, Turkey

The process of "letting go" starts even before I approach the entrance to the great Suleymaniye Mosque, the largest and most beautiful of the Imperial Mosques built during the time of the great sultan's rule over the vast Ottoman Empire. My surrender begins as soon as I hear the "call to prayer."

At the gate of the courtyard, I look up to the exquisite minarets and feel the stirring in my heart; I pause and take a deep breath, for I know what awaits me inside. I pass through the sunlit courtyard, stopping only to remove my shoes. The deep darkness of the inner mosque welcomes me as I find my place facing Mecca.

Then, from some forgotten memory, stored deep in the cells of my body, I lower myself to the floor: My knees touch the ancient Turkish carpet, hand woven by masters from another age, and my hands find their familiar position as finally my forehead touches the carpet. The surrender that first takes place in my mind and then in my heart is now complete within my body. One more time; I have answered the ancient call to come to this place. I have come to get my head to the floor so it is below my heart. Here; I am fully surrendered to God.

I continue to give myself over, trying again to let go of everything that I perceive the world is wanting from me. I begin to feel comfort from all of the prayers that have ever been offered here. As I take a deep breath and exhale, I feel myself sink even further into the exquisitely patterned carpet. I let go yet again and sense myself falling into the *invisible void that I know is my own "dark night of the soul."*

My first trip to Turkey changed my whole spiritual understanding. It was so much more than I ever expected or ever could have imagined. It was here that the veil that separated me from the Divine was lifted.

I had come to Istanbul to study Islamic mysticism, or Sufism as it is known in the West, with a teacher I had met at an international conference. He had arranged for the invitation. As with most Americans at that time, I knew next to nothing about Islam and actually very little about Sufism. Something within me urged me to accept this invitation. So it was in September of 1987 that I found myself on a United Airlines flight heading for Turkey.

If I had stayed in the States, I would have been returning for my second year of ministerial training. Even though the first year had gone well, it seemed to me that something was missing from the formal course of study. I was now meditating and praying on a daily basis but I seemed to be stuck on a plateau with my practice. It felt like I wouldn't be able to go any further without the guidance of a teacher—a special kind of teacher, one who knew the inner way.

I had previously experienced many great teachers and mentors who had taught me the lessons of the outer world. I remember them with fondness and respect. Now, though, I sensed that what I needed was much different. I needed the kind of teacher who understood the inner path to self-realization, the sort of teacher who comes to this life from a spiritual lineage that connects their soul to the invisible golden thread of true wisdom. The only thing I knew how to do was to pray for guidance and direction. And that I did. Finally, as always, the door was opened.

I probably wouldn't have spoken of it like this when it was actually happening to me. Only in retrospect do I see that I had longed for the inner life and was in search of someone who could guide me into it, beyond where I then stood. This was certainly not the work of ministerial training which, for the most part, had to do with teaching us about the "job" of running a church organization. Many of my classes had been about management and the techniques and ceremonies of ministering to others. In effect, it had little to do with the spiritual evolution of my soul. And this is what I wanted, what I was most seeking.

I had done a great deal of spiritual reading but never in the Islamic tradition. When this opportunity to study in Turkey presented itself, I knew I had to answer. I knew I had to go. It's as if the muezzin's call to prayer had traveled from Istanbul into my heart and beckoned me to come. And so I did.

Upon my arrival, I was immediately entranced by this wondrous city that was first called Byzantium, then renamed Constantinople at the beginning of the Christian era, and now Istanbul. It stands at the crossroads of East and West. It was here that I was to be introduced to the mystical truths of the Islamic faith.

Today, Istanbul, with its two bridges across the Bosphorus, connects the continents of Europe and Asia. The "look" is very Western, while the "feel" is Oriental. Walking down a side street or visiting a local cafe for the traditional Turkish coffee, it may be possible to observe people greeting each other by gently placing their hands on their chest over the heart area. This silent gesture means, "Welcome to my Heart." In essence, it symbolizes the great spirit of Sufi teachings.

Many Westerners have heard of Sufism through the great mystical writings of the 13th century poet Jelaluddin Rumi. Even so, few are aware that Sufism represents the mystical tradition of the Islamic faith as it has been passed down from the time of the Prophet Mohammed in the 7th century. All the world's great traditions have deep mystical tendencies, but these are often overshadowed by each religion's external formal organization and practices. In Islam, it was the Sufis who, over the centuries, sheltered and nourished the mystical aspects of the faith.

Soon after my arrival, I fell into a daily pattern of morning practice and study. My teacher had given me a couple of very good manuscripts in English about Islamic mysticism that had yet to be published in the West. These were to be my guide into what I would come to know as "the land of surrender."

My teacher was a university professor and had been initiated into more than one of the Sufi Orders. In addition, in the small town on the Eastern Black Sea where he had been raised, his father was known as a great Sufi healer. He really didn't attend school until he went to university for a law degree.

As a young boy, he had memorized the Holy Koran and been tutored in Arabic and French and later in English. But his true education came as he sat by his father's side, watching people come from far and wide to be healed. He told me that his most important lessons came when his father, in the course of working with a patient, would ask him, "Can you tell me what sort of thinking would show up as this kind of illness in the body?" In this way, his father was probing into the mind-body connection of healing long before we came to understand it in the West.

Because he knew the Holy Koran by heart, he was one of the reciters of it on Turkish national television for such special events as the commemoration of Mohammed's birthday. I loved hearing him recite. It was one of my favorite things. The flowing verses of the Koran spoken in the lilting sounds of Arabic would filter into my being.

I never understood what he was saying but I always had a closer sense of the presence of God when I gave myself over to hearing where the words were being spoken from. They came from across the desert and over the mountains from great and exotic lands. But, most importantly, they came from that cave on Mt. Hera where the Angel Gabriel first spoke them into Mohammed's soul. He memorized them. Others wrote them down. Again and again, people then gathered to hear the stories and the lessons spoken aloud. They began to organize their lives around what they were hearing. And, now in this special country of Turkey, I was receiving the gift of the sound of those same words.

Let me speak for a moment about revealed writings and sacred texts. It's been said the Divine's message has been revealed through a series of "best sellers" that were expertly suited to the particular culture, time, and people to which they were given. I've always liked that idea. And I've found a certain comfort in it. Over the years, I've been able to go to the writings of the sacred texts and be lifted up.

Whether it be the Darhmapada of Buddhism, the Holy Koran of Islam, the Bhagavad-Gita of Hinduism, the Torah of Judaism or the New Testament Gospels of Christianity, I have always found words of reassurance and comfort.

Visiting and praying in the mosques of Istanbul was an important aspect of my education there. The most famous of the city's mosques is the elegant Blue Mosque, so named for its priceless blue ceramic tiles that appear as jewels on its inner walls. It is truly an important and beautiful landmark, and it was the first mosque I prayed in after arriving in Istanbul.

But it was the Suleymaniye Mosque that made my heart sing. It was huge, the greatest and grandest of its time, even for hundreds of years after it was built in the 1550's. It is perched on one of the hills that you can see from most anywhere in Istanbul. It was the Suleymaniye that called to me. I loved its history. It was dark and worn and musty in a way that marks something that has been handed down for generations. It felt comfortable to me and became one of the places I visited when I wanted to settle deep into myself.

My teacher and I would go there often. I would sit and meditate off to the side while he would go down toward the front and begin the series of intricate postures that would make up one of the five daily prayer practices that would take his head to the floor in surrender to Allah, as the name of God was called in Arabic.

I never did learn the formal prayers of Islam. By the time I arrived in Turkey, I had my own prayer expression and meditation practice. However, it is important to note that aitislam means "surrender" in Arabic. In that sense, I somehow feel I got the essence of Islam through a deeper surrender into my own personal experience of the presence of God. That was its real gift to me.

Also, about once a week my teacher and I would visit a different mosque and he would instruct me on its history and unique features. After he had completed his prayers, we would sit quietly together on the carpet and discuss things of the Spirit. These were my lessons.

This is where questions were asked and answered.

When we would pray together in a mosque, we would sit off to the side of the main area. Usually, no one would bother to tell us to move to our appropriate places However, if there were several other men in the main area praying, I would quietly move to the more cloistered women's section.

Being a Western woman, there was part of me that resented having to move to the separated women's area. I didn't like it. It certainly wasn't what I was used to as a so-called "liberated woman." Then, my teacher told me a story about why it's this way. He said that the reason the women prayed behind the men is that they could do so and still keep their hearts and minds on God. However, the men weren't so blessed for, if they were to have to pray behind the women, they certainly wouldn't be able to keep their eyes, let alone their hearts, on God. In a simple but humorous sort of way, that had handled my protestations. Perhaps it was the beginning of my learning about surrender. Either way, I began to have respect for what my teacher and this tradition of practice was asking of me.

Sometimes, I would spend the afternoons walking the streets alone near my flat on the Asian side of Istanbul. I even liked to take a dolmish (a group taxi) to the harbor and get on a ferry that would carry me across the Bosphorus to the European side of Istanbul.

I loved being in the middle of the Bosphorus and looking in both directions—first to Asia and then to Europe. Either way I looked, I would see each side's hilly terrain and the minarets of the mosques. Oh, the minarets! There were literally thousands of them raising their elegant arms up to God.

On these afternoon ventures, I would also try to visit a mosque. Rarely did I attend formal prayers. Mostly, I went to sit and meditate. Then I would get my forehead to the floor and pray. I loved the beauty and the inner stillness that is found in most mosques.

On the Asian side, my favorite mosque was a new, bright, white marbled structure at Marmara University. It had a formal name which I could never remember because most people simply referred to it as the "faculty mosque." The floor was covered with a luxurious carpet that had been woven especially for it. The carpet was just breathtaking to behold, let alone walk on. In the afternoons, the sun would stream through the colored glass openings in its great dome. This is what I loved most. To sit and simply take in the rainbow of light that always welcomed me into its sacred dance.

It's now time for me to speak of the "eye of the heart." It was in Istanbul that I was first introduced to this most important spiritual idea. I'm not sure of its exact origin but I do know that it has woven its way through the spiritual tapestry of all the great mystical teachings. Here's how I understand it.

First, we are born into the world of opposites, which we learn to see through our two eyes. In fact, our two eyes duplicate the dual nature of the world in which we live. Thus, we learn to see dualistically without even knowing it. By this I mean that we learn to see things as either/or. In other words, we see things and conditions as black or white, good or bad, high or low, light or dark, right or wrong, and so forth. This is the realm of being into which we are born. It shapes us in ways we cannot even comprehend. Such dualistic seeing is the lens through which we experience the world.

As we continue to grow, we are constantly categorizing our experiences through this "invisible" lens of dualistic thinking. By the time we are teenagers, this mode of seeing the world is fully anchored in us, so much so that we aren't even aware of it.

Today, there are so many choices before us that it appears as if this dogmatic either/or option is fading away. But this is simply not the case. What we find today is a huge gray area between what was previously only black or white and good or bad. However, if you look closely, something of a much more subtle nature begins to arise. In the vast area of gray, we find a light gray and a dark gray. And if we examine our thoughts and beliefs even more closely, we would find a still finer light gray and a still softer dark gray.

No matter what it is we are viewing in the world, we are first seeing it through the "eyes" of dualistic consciousness. We may not always be aware of this but, at some level, it gets down to our either/or perception of reality:

If we bring awareness to this seeing, we may be able to look *through* the opposites to an ideal that is *beyond* the dual nature of our seeing. That which is beyond has been called by many names but they all point to the unitive realm of reality; that place or state of being in which everything is experienced as an eternal oneness. It exists beyond all belief and all ideas of separation. It is here we behold the Divine.

The first great world teacher who addressed this more universal way of seeing the world was Siddhartha Gautama, more commonly known as the Buddha, which means "The Awakened One." His own life serves as a living example to us all. Born a prince into a great and wealthy family, he left it all to become an ascetic, wandering around India with a begging bowl. Neither of these ways of living in the outer world answered his longing to know what was in his soul.

One day he sat under the now famous Bodhi Tree and looked into the nature of his own consciousness. It was an act of such single- minded courage. He sat there and waited... and watched. The resulting gift of this exploration became what is called the Royal Middle Way, the path of the Buddha. It is this movement in consciousness that everyone must embody on the journey toward the full realization of the One Life that is God known today as unitive consciousness.

Please note: I'm not saying everyone has to become a devotee of Buddha. I am saying that every individual's soul must receive the same realization into its nature as the Buddha did. Because he first did it and because so many others since him have done it, the path for us today is wider and the way is known.

The Buddha's great realization was that there is a place bigger than either/or that also includes the either/or. The teachings of the Buddha's Eight-Fold Path are the practices that take one on the journey to the Royal Middle Way. In other words, we are taken to a place in consciousness that allows us to see from a state of being that is unitive in nature. The highest principles or ideals that we know are born out of this universal unitive awareness in which there are no opposites. These ideals include such things as love, peace, freedom, wholeness and wisdom. They are the qualities and attributes that we most often assign to the Divine.

In the mystical traditions, this way of seeing has been associated with the third eye—that region in the center of the forehead that represents our highest mental functioning. Symbolically, it is where the two outer eyes become one inner eye.

It is from this invisible third eye that we seem to "know" more than we actually see. In other words, an inner way of viewing the world is developed that takes us beyond seeing just the appearances of the world. In a sense, when Jesus admonished his disciples to not judge by appearances, he was telling them to do the work of Buddha. (John 7: 24). It was as if he were asking them to get centered and see from within and then judge rightly, which can only be done from the unitive state of awareness we call Divine Love.

The opening of the third eye on the Royal Middle Way of practice is not the end of the work. After we begin to see and live from this more inclusive or unitive awareness, something else begins to stir. Only this time, it is in our hearts. The Buddhists often use the term "loving kindness" to describe what is being brought forth within this passage of our journey. Jesus called it "doing unto others that which we would want done unto us." (Matthew 7: 12}

What begins to take place in our awareness is described as the movement of the third eye into the heart. It's when the heart of compassion opens within us. It's as if this eye literally falls into our heart. And here, and only here, do we begin to see with the eye of love, the eye of wisdom and, yes, the "eye of the heart."

As I have studied the teachings and behaviors of Jesus, I came to see that he lived from this state of being. If the Buddha was awake, then Jesus was anointed. Jesus, The Anointed One, was anointed with the light and love of Christ. He lived from full Christ realization.

Because of this, he could "... heal the sick, cast out demons and raise the dead." (Matthew 1O: 8)

It's been said that we have to first become a Buddha before we can become a Christ. We have to be awake to see with the eye of unitive awareness. Just like I said, our souls must incorporate the awareness that the Buddha gave to humanity before it is prepared to engage the next step for our soul's evolution. We must come to know the anointing of love. Then, and only then, can we enter into seeing with the eye of the heart, the eye of love and the eye of compassion.

It's essential to make the following distinction about what often passes for compassion. I am not talking about sympathy. Usually, sympathy shows up when our unhealed hurt and pain gets activated when someone we see is hurting or in pain. At such times, we have actually projected our feelings onto the other. It's as if our unhealed "pains" and "hurts" connect with those of the other person. This is not what I'm pointing to here.

Seeing from the eye of the heart is like seeing from where the Divine sees. I believe it's where Jesus saw from. It is always a holy and sacred seeing. It is seeing from that which is whole in us. This seeing means we never feel the need to change anything, whether person, condition or circumstance. It only knows love, wholeness, joy and peace. Jesus said, "My peace I leave with you." (John 14: 27) When he said this, he was seeing from the Christ of his being. This is the nature we are called to duplicate. We are here to learn to see with the eye of the heart. To see from the Light and Love of the Truth of our being, which is the activity of God in us as Christ.

When I first came to know about the eye of the heart, I knew I had a long way to go. My practices of prayer and meditation were only the beginning of what would be asked of me. At least I had a glimpse into where I was being taken. It was another "peek" into what was being prepared for me.

That is, if I was willing to do the work and surrender yet again, to an even deeper realization, on this journey to the eye of the heart. Of course, there was that part of me that was all ready to begin. But, as with most passages on the path, there was a voice that said, "Well, look at all you've already done and experienced. Isn't that enough? Why don't you just relax here for a while? Haven't you worked hard enough?"

Then something happened that would guide my response to such questions. I was feeling restless. I had been in Istanbul a couple of months and wanted to get out of the city. The only other time I had traveled beyond the general vicinity of Istanbul was a wonderful trip up to the Black Sea coast shortly after I had arrived. So, one morning, I packed my bag and traveled south around the Sea of Marmara to the former capital city of Bursa. This city is known for its beauty and greenness. After getting settled into my hotel, I walked around the central part of the city and had some dinner.

Then, the first morning of the trip I got up about 4:30 a.m. to prepare for morning prayers. I had no idea where the local mosque was but I assumed I would be able to hear the call to prayer from my hotel room. I folded a blanket and placed it on the floor next to the wall. Then I proceeded to pull another blanket around my shoulders as I lowered myself to the floor. I was now ready to begin my surrender into meditation.

All of a sudden, the voice of the muezzin's invitation to prayer rang through my head. The loudspeaker must have been right outside my room. It was so loud! But in the next moment I heard an incredible sweetness to this voice that I had never previously experienced. The call rang through every cell of my flesh body. As he finished, it felt like I had been told that it was time for my life to be a prayer. No longer was I to simply pray. I was now to *become* the prayer.

In a sense, I had gotten my next assignment during that predawn call to prayer. My time in Istanbul would soon be coming to a close. But, one thing was for certain. I would be returning to America as a very different person from when I left. 1 would be returning with the knowing that my life was now God's life.

I knew I had to find a way to not only stay true to what had been given and opened within me while in Turkey, but also continue to make my way through the inner passage to the eye of my own heart. It was not going to be easy. I would face some of the most difficult challenges of my life. But, in some strange way, I had a sense that the *muezzin*'s voice from that morning's call to prayer would not leave or forsake me.

After this experience in Bursa, I realized I would have to face the places in me where I was still unhealed. Before my life in Istanbul would be complete, I would be taken through the greatest full surrender of myself to God that I had known up until that time.

For some days before this experience, I was struggling with my future plans. I knew that soon I would have to return to America, which meant I would also have to return to my husband and prepare the way for either our healing or our separation. I also had to know about the direction of my ministry. Was I to return to school and complete my course of study?

These were the thoughts that were pressing in on me as I took a taxi to visit my beloved "faculty mosque." Upon arrival, I walked over the elevated passage and through the courtyard that took me to the main entrance of this mosque. I placed my shoes on the shelf and walked up the circular staircase to the women's balcony. I had learned to appreciate being up here. Today, like most, I was by myself, for the formal prayers weren't scheduled for another couple of hours.

The sun shone its brightness upon the stained glass as I looked through the intricately carved marble lattice railing down into the expanse of the main mosque. My eyes were seduced by the colorful carpet. I noticed a couple of men going through the physical postures that form the rhythm of a devoted Moslem's prayer life. I gave them no thought as I sat cross-legged on the carpet. Contemplating, considering, thinking about my future, I sensed something stirring deep within me. I then realized that if I got on my knees and lowered my head to the floor there would be no turning back;

I paused, waiting. Finally, there was nowhere to flee, and nothing else to do. I found that familiar place facing Mecca and with my head to the carpet I began to pray in those now familiar words, "There is only One Life, this Life is God and this Life is Good and this Life is my life right now... "

My prayer continued to flow as I gave thanks for the lessons and blessings of the day and of my life, both in Turkey and in the United States.

Slowly, the "giving over" intensified as I repeatedly said, "I give my life to you... I give my ministry to You... I give my body to You..." On and on through everything I thought I was and everything that I thought I owned or controlled. I gave up past hurts and sorrows as well as successes and accolades. I gave up my attachments to people and my expectations of them. I gave up future dreams and goals yet unfulfilled. I even gave up my hopes and fantasies. And with each "giving up," the sobs grew deeper. The muscles in my body were convulsing with every word I spoke. Finally, I was spent. Everything had been given up—surrendered at the high altar of consciousness into this priceless Turkish carpet. There were no more tears. As I curled up in a fetal position, a gentle knowing washed through my soul, like a welcoming rain.

Eventually, I stood up and walked back out into my day. I didn't have any answers. I was drained. But I knew it would soon be time for me to return home to California and "clean up" my life. My soul had been emptied out in that mosque, and now I had to face returning home. I had to let Spirit begin to guide me as I prepared to walk through the affairs of my life.

Upon reflection, the greatest gift that I received from my study in Turkey was the importance of surrender. I know now that there is a place on the spiritual journey that all our inner progress is thwarted until we learn this most important practice. It's not easily taught in the West. Yet, for me, I'm eternally grateful for what was given and revealed to me during those three months in Istanbul. It made all the difference.

I returned to the United States and reentered the ministerial training program. My husband and I divorced but only after a year of healing and loving completion. He had been the person who first stood witness to my dream to be a minister and there were many times when he could see it for me when I couldn't see it for myself. At such times his support was invaluable. When I graduated from ministerial training, we were leading quite different lives. Even so, it was indeed a joyous day when he came to take me to lunch after I had passed my licensing panels.

That day our conversation was filled with laughter and gratitude. I truly felt blessed for all we had learned and shared together during the course of our marriage. Our lunch marked the closing of a door to an important part of my life. But, as always, I knew another was about to be opened. I was now ready to interview, or what is termed "candidate," for a senior minister position at a church.

One of the greatest things I took home with me from Turkey was the importance of connecting with one path from the teachings of the world's sacred tradition and practice it above all else. In other words, finding a truth teaching and giving yourself over to it is essential. You may, as I certainly did, explore different traditions or even different paths within a given tradition. However, there comes a time when I believe we must make a full commitment to a path, a teaching, a teacher and open our hearts to receive all that God has to offer through the discipline and revelations of that given path. It's how we each become disciples of truth.

Finally, we must always remember that, in the last analysis, all paths to God end in love. For love alone is where we are going. We may be traveling different "highways or byways" but we are all going to the same destination. This is what the mystics of every tradition have shown us.

After all the journeying, we end up in the "New Covenant" of love—the love that Jesus brought as the Christ to humanity. I came home to the Gospels, the "Good News" that proclaimed such a love. In particular, the Gospel of John lifted me up to the mystical reality of the Consciousness of Christ. It was St. Paul's teachings, in the Epistles of the New Testament, that showed me the possibility of my own relationship with the Risen Christ—that infinitely present activity of God that meets me in the eternal moment of now.

Whatever your path, if your intention to know God is pure and your desire to enter into love is sure, you will be guided. A way is always given. Little did I know that the door to the revelation of knowing Christ in my heart would be revealed inside a mosque in Istanbul! It is simply part of the great mystery of the spiritual pilgrimage. And what a mystery it is! I had been called into that dark and ancient mosque to be shown the way into the light of my own being. Yes, I had traveled to Turkey to be "Christed" in that mosque.

Practice:

The Love Prayer can be used to deepen our communion with God by simply "accepting and blessing" any intruding thoughts, feelings, and even physical pains as they arise.
- *Simply notice what is most attracting your attention. Is it a thought, a feeling, or a bodily sensation?*
- *Then use one of the following silent affirmations, coordinated with your breath:*
- *(Inhale) I accept this thought ... (Exhale) I bless this thought OR*
- *(Inhale) I accept this feeling ... (Exhale) I bless this feeling OR*
- *(Inhale) I accept this pain ... (Exhale) I bless this pain*

It's also helpful with the media. We all know certain individuals who regularly appear on television who upset us in some fashion. As a form of spiritual practice, you can tune to the programs where these people appear, and then attempt to really listen to them. If they are extremely upsetting to you, try turning off the sound and using the Love Prayer procedure until you are calm once again. Then, very gradually begin turning up the volume.

Once you have developed the capacity to listen to these upsetting individuals in a "mood of love," you have taken one more step towards finding heaven on earth.

Note: This practice is not intended to be used as a continuous affirmation or "mantra." It is to be engaged only as necessary to free your mind from any sort of internal or external distraction.

Chapter 7: Gratitude

The Cathedral
Seville, Spain

I feel comfort from all of the prayers that have ever been offered here. As I take a deep breath and exhale I feel myself sink further into the exquisitely patterned carpet. I let go yet again and sense myself falling into the invisible void that I know is my own "dark night of the soul"

Walking into the great Cathedral at Seville is much like walking into many of the other European cathedrals I had visited on previous trips, only this one is much more grand. It's filled with people speaking a variety of languages and I can feel my annoyance starting to rise from being in the midst of so many tourists in such a sacred place.

I try to get away from the crowds by visiting some of the side chapels off the main sanctuary. These twenty-seven small chapels each tell a story—of wealth, great art, and devotion to the Church by the leading families of the time who financed the construction of these chapels for personal family worship.

Finally, I find a quiet moment by the tomb of Christopher Columbus. I'm thinking about what he had to risk in order to explore the lands of the new world. This reminds me of all that I have endured on my own path of inner exploration.

I begin praying the Lord's Prayer. The words feel so new, so real, so full of life! It's as if I am praying this ancient prayer for the first time. I feel as though I am connecting with every person who has ever prayed this precious prayer. I hear myself say, "Yes... I am home in

Christ." Yet, more profoundly, I am aware that the Light of Christ is at home in me. Then I know that all I had sought outside of myself is now being revealed to me from within. The bell chimes again. I welcome this new awareness of being at home in Jesus Christ—right here in this grand cathedral and most importantly, in the heart of my being.

The ancient Church of Seville was so lovely! It's opened my heart again just to remember the beauty. There's just something wonderful about the early European cathedrals that still call the faithful. They were built over long periods of time by many people, coming from all walks of life, seeking inner peace.

I've always been at peace in these great old Cathedrals. I'm grateful that I've had the opportunity to visit these ancient places. I continue to carry them in the center of my heart. I now know that their expression has added greatly to my experience in the world.

Each of them was built with such love, by people who understood that what they were building with stone was a mirror of what they were building in their heart – it was part of their spiritual practice.

Let's look at the whole arena of spiritual practice. First of all, spiritual practice, especially prayer and meditation, is the time we spend each day devoted to developing a greater awareness of God in our lives. It has no other activities mixed in with it. During our times of practice, we are being asked to give our full attention exclusively to God. That is to say, you can't really meditate while you're driving a car, even though one of my former students said he did it all the time!

People have often asked, "How much time should I spend in my daily practice?" As I've already said, in the beginning stages of my practice, I was willing to spend five minutes. Very soon though, I was able to increase the amount of time I devoted each day to my practice. It's really your decision to choose the amount of time that works for you. I would, however, suggest that it's better to start with a few minutes a day on a regular and consistent basis than to attempt a longer period of time that would be more difficult to sustain.

One of the great understandings of the last hundred years has been the idea that thoughts are creative and, therefore, what we think matters. This is now being seen throughout our culture. Just go into the "self-help" section of any book store and you will see that much of what is being written focuses on the power of our thoughts – the power of right thinking to change our lives, to transform our relationships and even to heal our bodies.

Through prayer, our words become containers for God's power. Our words are creative and are then filled with life giving energy. In this way, we can again see that our time spent in spiritual study and practice can change our thinking and transform our lives.

It is written that the truth will make you free. (John 8: 32) But I would add, "... not the truth about someone else but the truth about ourselves." For each of us, alone, is the only person who can ultimately do the work that sets us free from our own self-defeating behaviors and patterns. All such patterns keep us bound to ignorance, fear, and suffering.

This work of being set free first takes place at the psychological level of our being and then progresses to the more spiritual levels of awareness. For me, one of my great realizations was that the healing I had done at the psychological level assisted me in being more functional and successful in the world. But the work at the spiritual level set my soul free for all eternity.

This kind of spiritual healing meant that my freedom no longer depended upon the conditions or circumstances of my life in the world but was, in fact, rooted in the Divine. My inner happiness no longer depended upon who called or what I received in the mail that day. I also came to realize that I was responsible for my own reactions to whatever was before me, to whatever happened in the course of any given day.

Seen in this light, our spiritual practice may be the most important thing we can *do* each day to experience greater freedom in our lives. Yes, in this work we *are* asked to do something. However, though our first response may be to want to go out into the world and change others, in the spiritual life, we are first and foremost called to change ourselves.

This is not easy, as was evidenced by one of the participants in a retreat I was facilitating. When I would speak about the importance of having a spiritual practice, he would raise a question about needing to do something in the world. This went on for a couple of days, until I finally said, "Praying and meditating *is doing* something!" Well, the light bulb went off in his head and he realized what we had been talking about. This was his first step in fully understanding that the real work is in taking responsibility to change first ourselves and then serve the world from this new, enlightened awareness.

For example, each time we meditate, we have the opportunity to discern the errors and falsehoods that exist within our thought patterns. Once we can see and name them, we are free to release and change them. Very often these error patterns have affected whole areas of our lives. One that I discovered was my deeply held belief that I had to "work hard for money." Eventually this belief "took form" in my being what is termed a "workaholic." Because of this behavior and the belief that was operating behind it, I repeatedly experienced times filled with effort and struggle in my work life. This pattern was very difficult to break because its very existence was rewarded by my employers. Yes. What was ultimately harming me, was seen as being "good" for the companies that employed me. In some cases, I was a model of success for them.

This reminds me of the story of Joseph as it is recorded in the Bible. He was the youngest of the twelve sons of Jacob and Rachel and was the son to whom Jacob had given the beautiful "coat of many colors." (Genesis 37: 3) His brothers were very angry and jealous and eventually conspired to abandon him for dead in a cistern in the desert. But before Joseph was about to die, he was discovered by a traveling caravan and taken into Egypt. It was here that he grew strong and thrived and eventually became a close advisor to the Pharaoh.

Meanwhile, several famines had come to the land of Canaan, where his "long lost" family members were still living. Due to these famines, his father had sent ten of his brothers into Egypt in search of food. Because of Joseph's position in the government, they would have to interact with him in the purchase of these desperately needed food supplies. The brothers didn't even recognize Joseph when they began their bargaining but he recognized them. Eventually, the family was reunited and Joseph was able to visit with his elderly father before his death.

What's been important to me about this story is Joseph's response to his brothers. He didn't get mad at them; in fact, he was very forgiving. He was genuinely happy to see them. Furthermore, he didn't carry a grudge or end up living as a "victim." Instead, he took responsibility for his own experience and created a new life for himself in Egypt. He achieved what I would call a "higher" understanding. This is demonstrated by what he said to his brothers, "...you thought evil against me; but God meant it for (my) good."(Genesis 50:20)

I have often returned to this story for guidance. One example took place during the second year of my pulpit ministry, when I could see that I would "burn out" if I continued working the long hours that I thought were required of me. I was becoming a victim of my work. Finally, I realized something had to change and that the "something" had to be me. I began working with my Spiritual Director to "un-pack" the error belief of having to work extra hard to be successful.

Like Joseph, there was no one to blame or to condemn. Not even myself. I had been doing the best that I could and the best that I knew how to do, given my awareness and skills at the time. However, there were things for me to now see and understand about my thoughts, beliefs and choices. My daily practice of meditation and prayer opened those up for me.

The more we engage in a daily, dedicated spiritual practice, the more our lives will be guided and directed from within. This is what happened to the Prophet Elijah when he heard the "...still small voice." (I Kings 19: 11-12) Today we call this voice of inner guidance our intuition. This voice of intuition only speaks to us in the present moment. It simply cannot speak through the past memories or the future fantasies that live within our minds. As it has been said, probably thousands of times, the only reality is the now moment.

The voice of God that we call the still small voice or the voice of intuition reveals itself in different ways to each of us. For some, it comes as a felt experience of the Holy Presence that guides us. For others, it may show its guidance as a symbol or an image. For still others, it comes as a voice from deep within.

For me, it usually comes as a voice but I have to ask for its guidance to hear it.

I usually do this by first getting quiet and prayerful. Then I simply ask, in the name of God or the Presence of Christ, if it is right for me or is it wise for me to... (place your words in here) ... Then I listen.

Most often, it responds as a quiet voice that appears to be at the lower right back of my head area.

I learned through trial and error not to ask for guidance around petty or seemingly little things. Instead, I held this process sacred and would generally only ask for what was mine to do in any situation or opportunity that was before me, especially in regard to my ministry.

The most important things I've learned about my relationship with this presence, this voice, is that I had to first call upon it. I had to be the one to initiate my relationship with it. It only goes where it's invited. That's right; it comes by invitation only.

I've also learned that this precious voice doesn't get louder but it does get clearer as we grow and strengthen in our faith through dedicated daily spiritual practice. It reveals itself as a result of our own inner preparation. Such preparation is demonstrated through our devotion to our own spiritual practice. Over the years, I came to know this voice as the indwelling presence of the activity of God that is Christ within each individual's soul.

The way of the world seems to ask us to keep a score card that tally up the things we accumulate whether it be awards, trophies, recognition, money, houses, success, or whatever. There's lots of agreement in the world for doing just this. As I said, throughout most of my early life it seemed as if these things were all that mattered. The pressure to have them seemed so real and so powerful. Yet it all came down to one question. With each single step I was taking on the spiritual path, I was being asked to choose between the pull of needing these things from the world and the call of the still small voice within. And we know what choice the great spiritual masters who have gone before us, all made.

All of this is why dedicated spiritual practice is so essential.

Each of us needs daily time to commune with God; to speak through prayer and to listen through meditation. Daily practice exposes the insidious pull of the world and gives us the opportunity to develop our spiritual "seeing." It supports us in making the kinds of choices that keep us on the path and draw us nearer to the reality of God. It's where we enter into a state of God-communion and thereby realize a greater sense of our unity with the infinite and abundant nature of the Divine.

I remember a time in meditation when I wanted to understand what Jesus meant when he said, "But seek first the kingdom of God and his righteousness, and all these things shall be added to you." (Matthew 6: 33) I had worked with this scripture in prayer and meditation for about three years. I had prayed it, studied it, and wrestled with it. Finally, the light of understanding broke through one day as I was getting out of my car in a parking lot in Sausalito, California.

I stood beside the car and looked up at the deep blue sky on the near perfect San Francisco Bay Area day. I started to laugh. I "saw" that once I had experienced this promised kingdom at the inner level of my being, the "things of the world" would pale by comparison. It simply wouldn't matter In that instant, I also saw how much these "things" had driven my life, shaped my relationships, competed for my attention and had even stolen my vitality and aliveness. It seemed as if these things were what had mattered most to me.

It's not easy to confess just how much this need for the things of the world had run my life. But on that sunny day in Sausalito, I had entered another room in the many mansions of consciousness. Just as Jesus had promised; "In my Father's house are many rooms; if it were not so, I would have told you. I go to prepare a place for you." (John 14: 2) In this new room of awareness, the "world" hardly mattered. At least I could finally see my needs for what they were.

This need for the things of the world had formed the necessary experiences that were designed to assist me on my own "hero's journey" to self-actualization. Going for them is how I developed the skills to have mastery over my world. But God's promise through Jesus had to do with the inner life, and in that parking lot I had just been invited into that new room of the kingdom.

The great paradox is that as we keep our thoughts on God, as our "eye is single," everything we need from the world is provided. It is given to us exactly on time and in exactly the right amounts and with more than enough to share.

But I caution you that it will not always fit your previous "pictures" of how you thought it would look.

The thing I learned that day, and now know fully for myself, is that we are always being provided for—no matter what comes our way. It would take me another few years to fully integrate what I saw that day in Sausalito. Even now; this experience continues to guide my life and enrich my spiritual practice.

Daily dedicated spiritual practice also reveals the many gifts of God's loving presence in our lives. We can only know this presence through our own individual consciousness. No one else can know it for us, just as no one else can ever do our practice for us. Sure, we can look to others as examples or for inspiration and guidance along the way but, in the final analysis, the indwelling presence can only be fully realized within the very heart and center of our own being; through our own reality, our own self, our own individuality. Yes, we are the only person who can be responsible for what we bring to our relationship with the Holy Presence of God.

And today, after all my journeys, after all my seeking, I have come home to Jesus Christ. The Universal Light of Christ is now individualized "at home" within me, in the cathedral of my heart.

Practice:

Start a daily spiritual practice.

What do we mean when we say 'daily dedicated spiritual practice'?

Daily, dedicated spiritual practice is the time that is spent each day exclusively devoted to developing a greater awareness of God in your life. It is the time spent in meditation, prayer and spiritual study. Although it is desirable to bring a spiritual perspective into every activity that you engage in, <u>dedicated practice has no other activity mixed in with it.</u> Don't delude yourself with rationalizations such as, "I kind of meditate while I'm mowing the lawn." While that may be true, it is <u>not</u> 'dedicated spiritual practice.'

Chapter 8: Sorrow

Mary's House
Ephesus, Turkey

Leaving the old city of Ephesus, I'm quiet and serene in my seat. I'm riding the bus that's winding its way up the old road to the top of Nightingale Mountain. I am returning to one of the most sacred places I have ever experienced—the house of the Virgin Mary. It's the little stone structure where she lived and supported St. John's ministry to the people of this region now known as Asia Minor.

It's been nearly seven years since my first visit here and this is the place where I began opening my heart to Blessed Mother Mary. It's also where I was guided and shown the direction for the next unfoldment of my ministry.

These thoughts fill my mind as I leave the bus and proceed reverently up the olive tree-lined cobblestone walk that will take me, once again, into Mary's heart.

My eyes are starting to tear as I feel the tug to "let go." By the time I enter the door of the little cottage, I'm sobbing. I find my place sitting on the only chair in the small room that is now a shrine.

It seems as if a well of sadness has burst forth from deep within my soul. I look to the altar and see the statue of Mary. with the beautiful flowers that have been placed at her feet. I smell the sweet incense that fills the air. Through the small window, the bright afternoon sun pierces the shadows of the room. Blessed be Mary, whose own tears have come across the centuries to mix with mine. The flames of the prayer candles are dancing in the presence of the divine love that is the nature of her being.

I close my eyes and attempt to reach within for some deeper knowing. All the while, tears continue to cascade down my face. Just when I am about to give up hope that the sobs will end, I feel a light touch on my arm. The priest, who was attending to the room when I arrived, gently whispers, "Your tears are precious to Mary."

I had cried too, the first time I visited Mary's House in Turkey. Only that time the tears were of uncertainty and confusion for what I was struggling with regarding my spiritual life. I was feeling raw and opened as I rode on the bus coming down from her house that day of my first visit there. Then, all of a sudden, the "voice" of the Lord spoke to me in a way I will never forget. It seemed to explode in my head and said, "Start the church in my name." I knew exactly what it meant. Prior to that trip, I had been praying and pondering about my ministry. Specifically, I was wondering what my next step was to be. I had been feeling torn inside between what I called the "outer" and the "inner" church.

I had enjoyed a certain success in the building of the outer church. I loved preparing and giving the Sunday talks as well as teaching classes and workshops. But the outer church had many other demands and responsibilities. I was tired of the amount of time and attention it took to manage a large church organization and monitor its financial well-being. The inner call for a closer walk with the Divine seemed to come in second to the more pressing needs of a public ministry.

I wanted a contemplative spiritual experience, and the guidance I received coming down the mountain confirmed this. I knew it was time to leave the outer church and begin the deep and long process of building the inner temple within my own being. I had no idea what this new direction would look like, nor did I know where to begin. But I did know that I had to respond to what was a clear directive to my soul. It would be the biggest single step of faith I had ever taken.

After returning home from that trip, I announced to my congregation that in six months I would be resigning my position as their senior minister. I asked them to enter into a completion process and assured them that at the end of our time together they would have their new minister. I trusted I would also be guided in my own next steps.

From my past experiences, I knew first hand that incomplete endings inhibit new beginnings and that good completion with the minister who was leaving makes all the difference in how a church community welcomes a new minister. I told the congregation that our completion work together would serve them personally by providing an opportunity to complete "unfinished business" with past relationships or even with loved ones they had lost. I knew it would be an important few months for us. Perhaps it would even be the most important time we would spend together in the course of my being their minister.

I was reflecting on all of these things as well as the other changes in my life that followed my first trip here as I began walking up the cobblestone path to that sacred house for the second time. Over the ensuing years, I had done much of the work of building my own inner temple. It's really not that we build it but rather that we build a pathway into knowing this part of our being. It's the part that I believe has always existed through the long evolution of our souls. It's the part that continues even after we lay down the physical flesh body.

What I'm referring to is sometimes called the true self or the higher self, or the indwelling Christ. There's a movement on the spiritual path where we begin to merge with it and become more like it until, finally, we are fully unified with it. It's as if these two parts of ourselves, the human personality and the true self, become one. Traditionally, this is what has been called the "mystical marriage" of Christ in the soul.

This unfolding process asks much of us. First, what we might call the false self or the human personality must be carefully dismantled. This doesn't happen overnight. In fact, to try to do so would be very destructive. However, as we continue in our spiritual work and practice, we grow in strength and awareness and find ourselves releasing old beliefs and behaviors. We experience greater freedom as attachments and dependencies begin to fall away. We lay down judgments and find that even some of our friendships may end. We also find that the things that used to create fun and excitement for us now seem empty. Finally, we discover that we are being transformed from the inside out. In other words, we find ourselves "walking the talk" of a spirit-led life.

Believe me, I know it is much easier to talk about than to actually do. Yet this is why I left pulpit ministry. I wanted to walk the deep walk with the Divine. I wanted to speak from my own realization rather than repeating someone else's story or quoting their good ideas. I wanted to know for myself what it would mean to experience the living presence of God as an inner and eternal reality.

Anyhow, by my second visit to Mary's House, I had pretty much settled into a private form of ministry. I lived and worked out of a loft in Portland, Oregon and taught classes and workshops while consulting and developing programs for churches. In addition, I served as spiritual director to other ministers. I also met weekly in a prayer circle with a few companions on this inner way.

I was enjoying a more integrated and conscious life than I had ever known. However, there were areas within me that still hadn't been brought to the Light. I had to be willing to face those parts of me that resisted being transformed. It was to be a very difficult passage in my spiritual life. Things such as separation, judgment, and fear would creep to the surface of my mind from the most dark and silent recesses of my awareness. And then, if out of nowhere, the sorrow would emerge.

When these feelings got stirred up, my survival strategy was to "take control." And it really didn't matter what I controlled. It could be a project I was working on or a person's behavior. It often showed up while standing in line at the post office or the grocery store! Whatever activated such feelings didn't really seem to matter. The important point was that during these times, I was being shown that I still had lots of work to do. It kept me humble. It announced I had so much more to learn about "unconditional" love. Love without conditions. Love free from judgment, dependency, compulsivity, and suffering.

It was during this second trip to Mary's house that I faced what would become the next great movement of my journey. I had come here to find out if I was willing to go the whole way with love. Was I really willing to allow love to have its way with me and through me? Just like after the first time at Mary's House, I didn't know where to begin. I sensed it would take all the faith I had and then some.

Perhaps the only thing I knew is that I was willing. Yes, I was willing. I had to remember that my willingness was my worthiness. If I was truly willing, I trusted I was worthy of knowing the blessings of God's many promises of love. Slowly, I began to accept that I was worthy of knowing the kind of love that Jesus had demonstrated over and over again in his short ministry.

I also sensed that I would be changed, or, if you will, made new again, in my walk towards love. I also felt there would be yet other people, things and habits that would have to be laid down. All I knew is that here I was, once again, saying "I'm willing, show me the way." So began the dark night of my soul's passage to the power and presence of Divine Love.

Not having been raised Catholic, Mother Mary was not part of my early religious experience. Of course, she was always present at Christmas as the young virgin giving birth to Jesus. Other than that, she was a mystery. But, again, oh what a mystery! Little did I know that one day she would come to me speaking "words of wisdom" just as Paul McCartney's song had promised.

For me, Mary has come to represent the feminine face of God. She's not the first to do so. There were others before her; Isis in Egypt, Artemis in Greece, who was called Diana by the Romans, Shakti in Hinduism, Quan Yin in China, and Sophia in the Jewish wisdom teachings. Mary herself is a rare gem with many facets. I have experienced but a few of these. First, of course, is the beginning image that most people raised in the Christian faith remember. It's the one that depicts an innocent virgin watching over the newborn babe in the manger.

As I'm writing this, it's Christmas Eve and I'm spending the week at a Trappist Abbey in Oregon. Earlier today in the little chapel of this monastery, I saw the familiar crêche scene that epitomizes this image of her. I will soon attend the midnight mass that heralds the story of the birth, told across the generations. This is the Mary I knew as a child. But just as this nativity scene will be boxed up and put away, so too did I do the same with Mary when I left the church all those many years ago.

I'm reminded of a scripture in the New Testament that asks us to be about the Father's business. (Luke 2: 49) But, it ends there. It doesn't quite tell us exactly what it means or how to do it. One day I realized that the way we go about the Father's business is by expressing the Mother's nature. Wow! That woke me up!

By that time in my studies, I had come to accept that the Father principle was the all-pervading life force and intelligence of the universe. But what was the Mother's nature? How was I to learn about it? I began to see that the Mother's nature is how the Father principle gets expressed in the world. This is why the Holy Spirit is sometimes viewed as the feminine aspect of the Trinity. In other words, Mary, the Holy Spirit, is forever giving birth to the Son of the Father in us. This Son is the consciousness of Light, of Christ, that was present in our souls from the beginning. It's how heaven comes to earth right where we live, right in the seat of our own individual awareness.

To arrive at such an exalted understanding, I first had to ask, "Just what is the Mother's nature?" This was a hard question for me. My background in higher education and in business was during the growth of the women's liberation movement. Though not involved in it as such, my struggle to compete in the world and earn my so-called place at the table of success mirrored much of what has been written about this movement in the 1970s and early 80s.

In order to have done what I did, I had left behind a lot of ideas and images of what my grandmother and mother knew and accepted about being a woman. When I sought to understand, let alone experience, the Mother's nature, there were few places for me to turn. I was afraid of what I would see and I feared what I would have to face about myself. I somehow sensed there was a big piece of me that had been buried and denied in order to have a successful career.

In some ways, I'm not really sure how my journey to Mary began. A couple of instances come to mind. It was about my second year in the ministry when one of my congregants invited me to take the day and drive down to a famous bookstore in Palo Alto, California. There was a feeling of tranquility as I walked through the many small rooms that comprised its extended structure.

Usually, books sort of jump right out at me, at least the ones I'm supposed to add to my library. Nothing like that happened to me that day, except for one curious thing: I kept being drawn back to a large lighted case that held sacred objects and jewelry from the world's various religious traditions. Along with many other kinds of prayer beads, there was a beautiful sterling silver rosary with amethyst beads. I had never had a rosary and didn't even know how to use one. Somehow, it didn't matter. It was the only thing I bought that day.

For years this rosary just sat on the table next to my meditation chair. I would pick it up occasionally and run the little beads between my fingers, wondering if perhaps someday I would know what to do with it. A couple of years after I acquired the rosary, a dear friend gave me a simple, modernized clay sculpture of Mary as a Christmas gift. It was different from any other I had ever seen. I placed it near the rosary on my altar. As I think back about it, it feels as if Mary was always there with me, just waiting and sort of standing watch. I would notice her from time to time but she hadn't been invited into my heart. That is, not yet. My invitation to her was going to be a slow and gradual process.

About the same time, something else began to happen. While shopping at the local super market, I ran across the beautiful tall glass Mary candles, the kind that are usually imported from Mexico and end up as part of shrines in people's living rooms. One day I bought one and put it on my bedside table. I began lighting it before I went to bed. Often, I would just look at it, say some prayers, blow it out, and go to sleep. At other times, I found myself waking up in the middle of the night to its soft glow. No one knew I was doing this. It's something I held very private. I couldn't explain, even to myself, how I was ending up with Mary in my life. I was keeping her at arm's length, but it was comforting to have her in my house.

Move ahead a decade and I'm in Paris for the Christmas holidays. I went to visit the world-famous Chartres Cathedral, which I had never before seen.

No words can really do justice to its exquisite stained-glass windows which, centuries ago, served to tell the major stories of the Bible to its illiterate congregation. The cathedral is also known for the labyrinth formed in stone on its main floor. It was covered with pews at the time of my visit so I wasn't able to walk it as I had done with the other modern replicas that are now available in the United States.

The thing I remember most about my visit to Chartres was a regally dressed statue of the Black Madonna. Sitting before this symbolic representation of Mary, I began to wonder what her message was to me. I lit a couple of prayer candles situated beneath her high perch and then walked out into the gray overcast winter day. I took with me a sweet sense of her goodness.

I've also visited Mary in the little stone church where Christopher Columbus and his sailors said their final prayers before setting out to discover the New World. This island of La Gomera, one of the smallest of the Canary Islands, is located in the Atlantic Ocean off the African coast of Morocco. It's part of Spain and was Columbus' last stop in order to restock his ships with supplies and fresh water before the long adventure that would bring him to the Americas.

There's also another, more famous, Mary on the Canary Island of Tenerife. It's the Black Madonna shrine in the village church of Candelaria. I visited both of these Marys during my two-week stay on the islands.

Then in the fall of 2001, I was putting together a small group of people to travel to Portugal the following May. One of the highlights of the trip would be a pilgrimage to the shrine of Mary at Fatima. A few months before our departure, I had finally learned how to pray the rosary. I changed some of the phrases to fit with my own understanding, but left its essence intact. I started praying the rosary beads before going to sleep and noticed that if something had troubled me during the day, I would often get some guidance, or even an answer, during these evening prayers.

Starting the practice of saying the rosary is what prepared me for my visit to Fatima on the anniversary of Mary's May 13 appearance to the three shepherd children in 1916. I entered the massive courtyard of the shine with more than 6,000 other pilgrims from around the world. I lit candles, prayed in one of the side chapels and listened to the outdoor Mass being recited in four different languages. I stood in awe as pilgrims who had walked for weeks came down the central aisle. Many were even crawling on their hands and knees.

One mother was carrying her child who was too deformed to walk. It was here that my sense of Mary's presence and love became fully alive, and where my devotion to what she represents became sure within me.

Portugal's churches are filled with statues of what I began to call "Fatima Marys." These statues portray Mary in a distinct way from others I had seen around the world. This unique Mary regally stands with her beautiful golden and jeweled crown as "Queen of Heaven." In each and every church we visited, she was prominently displayed with fresh roses or rose petals surrounding her feet. To me, she's the face of the glorious Mother Mary.

I've also encountered another face of Mary, known as Our Lady of Guadalupe. She's portrayed quite differently from those I saw in Portugal. It was outside of Mexico City that she revealed herself to Juan Diego, a recently widowed (and baptized) peasant man in 1531. This face of Mary has a humbleness about it. The Trappist Abbey that I'm writing this chapter in is named for her. Both in the chapel and in my retreat room, I've studied her picture and surrendered into the sweetness of her face.

Whatever facet of Mary is shown to me, I'm reminded of how much sorrow she has lifted from my life. That's her job, of course. Yes, it's the Mother's nature that leads us through the passage of sorrow on our spiritual sojourn through the dark night of the soul. This sorrow isn't a sadness associated with any particular hurt or grievance. Instead, it's like a deep well that bubbles up from the depths of the body.

I remember saying to my friend who was also going through this passage, "Where is this coming from?" At that time, neither one of us had an answer, but we both felt it had a lot to do with Mary. I sensed it represented the sorrow that comes from across lifetimes. It's the kind of sorrow that is reflected in ignorance and nurtured through hate, anger, judgments, condemnations and anything else that separates us from Divine love. Mary has born such sorrow and because of this, her gift to me is that I'm not alone. She became my teacher, ushering me into the realm of the Universal Mother.

It is written that she was a virgin. Just what could this possibly mean? I believe that being a virgin really meant, at the highest level of seeing, that she had a purified soul. In other words, she lived from a pure "womb" of consciousness that was prepared to bring forth the chosen one. The mystery behind the term is that she had a pure heart, a virgin heart, if you will. In other words, I feel that love flowed so freely in her heart that when the Angel of the Lord appeared before her, she didn't waiver. Instead, she said "yes" to God. She didn't tremble. She was willing. She stood faithful. She accepted her assignment with grace.

I began to ask myself, "What needs to be purified in me so that love can have a greater expression through me, in service to the revelation of the Light in humanity?" As I asked this question on my journey to Mary, she has answered. She shows me that the love that moved through her could be invited to move through me. Again, I knew I had to ask. This meant another surrender. Then I wonder if I'm worthy of such Love. I didn't really know but, as before, I am willing. I began moving closer to her and identifying with her.

I wanted to understand her special gift to humanity. Daily I prayed, "Blessed Mary, purify my soul with your Love so that Christ may be glorified in my flesh."

As with Jesus, I came to realize that what was flowing through the Holy Mother was more important than the religious doctrines that evolved out of her historical life. It was revealed to me that Divine Love was moving and living itself through her. Divine Love was so fully present within her that she was the one to birth Jesus and thus bring forth the light and love of Christ into the world.

As I moved more deeply into the mystery of Mary, I discovered how little I'd actually known about love. For example, once when I was facilitating a healing service for the leadership team of another minister's church, I had the strange sensation that a part of my consciousness was in each person's soul. Yes, it seemed as if the light in me was shining itself into the dark rooms of their unconsciousness. And all the while the Spirit of Mary was whispering to my heart with the words, "Just love them... Just love them." It was as if I were being guided to love the darkness, the error, and the unconsciousness in each person. I was humbled because I knew it was the most holy thing I would ever do in that room with those gathered before me.

In a sense, it's what Mary did as she stood witness to the persecution of her beloved son. There was still room in her "immaculate heart" to love the unconscious darkness that was being played out through all of the people who participated in his crucifixion. Love knew in her that there was more to be given, more to be revealed. Standing in that healing service, I knew that behind the darkness was the Light of lights waiting to be called forward.

Did Mary know that the Light would bring forth a resurrection? I don't know. However, I do know that Love did. And because Love did, she had the courage and the faith to be open to Love's ultimate expression through her. Love used her then and it continues to use her spirit now to teach us how to love. Yes, Mary's spirit of love is teaching me more about Love itself.

I began to wonder, "What is it that Mother Mary can say to me as I long to bring forth a greater and fuller revelation of the living Christ within my being?" She responded by saying that three qualities—love, strength and faith—must be realized and nurtured in my soul in order for me to take the journey through the dark night and be resurrected by the Light. I knew that's where I wanted to be. Today, I also feel and believe that it's the destiny for each of us. It's the Divine Plan that has been in place from the beginning.

I've tried to imagine what it must have been like for her to enter into such love at Jesus' birth and such sorrow at his crucifixion. What strength of heart did it take for her to stand witness to her son's death? Surely, over the years, she had gone through many phases of letting him go, of releasing him, so that his life could serve a greater purpose in their world. What faith did it take, knowing that she had birthed a "chosen one," only to stand there at the foot of Calvary and see him rejected, betrayed, and seemingly forgotten? And then to be raised up to the joy of his resurrection!

Yes, she tells me that this process is a passage for each of us. First, we must love in order to enter into the awareness of Christ. Then, the sorrow rips us open as we witness our own ignorance and error. We feel the pain of the breaking up of attachment and false dependency to the things of the world. It is here that death seems so inviting, so real. The dark night of the soul is truly upon us. But death is not the final plan. It is simply not to be.

Eventually, the lightness of joy breaks forth as Christ is resurrected anew in us. Actually, it is in this that we become its greater expression in the world.

Just as Jesus appeared to the disciples to anoint them in the light and love of Christ so that they could go forth to minister the "good news," so we are called to be anointed in the truth of Christ within us. Such a path we travel!

Love calls us to this journey and it takes enduring strength to continue through the many "deaths" of our life experiences. But, slowly—step by step--our faith is established and grows, as the call of the inner life is greater than the pull of the outer world.

This is exactly what Mary faced at the foot of Calvary. She stood there, seeing what the world had delivered. Yet, somewhere from deep within her being, the strength and faith that had been practiced over the years carried her forward. Perhaps she found solace in those precious words spoken by the Angel Gabriel nearly three decades earlier; "Greetings, you who are highly favored! The Lord is with you. Do not be afraid, Mary, you have found favor with God." (Luke 1: 28 & 30) Today, I know that each of us is "highly favored" on our journey. Those words spoken to Mary are really promises of God for us this day. May we find solace in them too!

I continue to call on Mary's love to find my strength, to expand my faith and to realize the risen Christ within my very own being. I also claim and know it for all of us. Resting in this awareness, the familiar prayer, first prayed over a thousand years ago, beckons me... "Hail Mary, full of Grace, the Lord is with thee. Blessed art thou among women and blessed is the fruit of thy womb, Jesus." (Luke 1:42)

Whether it be the Virgin-with-child Mary, the Black Madonna, Fatima Mary or the Our Lady of Guadalupe, each of these, as well as the many other faces of Mary, are representations of the Universal Mother's nature that is the feminine face of God. In this Mother's womb we are delivered up to Love.

And the Holy Mother's Love is among us. A new room in the many mansions has been opened to me. It has been opened for all of us. What moved through Mary is moving through us right now. Our work is to consciously duplicate it in our lives. The Angel Gabriel, who first appeared to Mary, stands before each of us saying, "You are highly favored... blessed is your life." How are we to answer? Are we willing to be a center for love to enter the world?

Be careful not to answer too soon. Pause. Pray. Meditate. Look within... for I can tell you it's the single most difficult spiritual practice to which I have been called.

However, today I know there's no other place to go. This is where the sorrow I experienced at Mary's house has led me. It continues to teach me that Love is all there is.

Practice:

Consider an image of Mary, the mother of Jesus – maybe several – and contemplate what her experience must have been, and then ask: "What is it that Mother Mary can say to me as I seek to bring forth a greater and fuller revelation of the living Christ within my being?"

When we do this work, it's as if these two parts of ourselves, the human personality and the true self, become one. Traditionally, this is what has been called the "mystical marriage" of Christ in the soul.

The Angel Gabriel, who first appeared to Mary, stands before each of us saying, "You are highly favored... blessed is your life." How are we to answer?

Are we willing to be a center for love to enter the world?

Be careful not to answer too soon. Pause. Pray. Meditate. Look within... for I can tell you it's the single most difficult spiritual practice to which I have been called.

> *Hail, Mary, full of grace, the Lord is with you.*
> *Blessed are you among women,*
> *and blessed is the fruit of your womb, Jesus.*
> *Holy Mary, Mother of God, pray for us*
> *now and at the hour of our Resurrection.*

Chapter 9: Communion

The Upper Room
Jerusalem, Israel

Approaching the whitewashed house, I pause to take a deep breath before passing through the old iron gate. Only after becoming fully present to this moment do I begin to climb the steps that will take me to the room that has filled my thoughts for months. Each step brings me closer to realizing my dream. Here I am, about to enter the "upper room" where it is believed that Jesus participated in the Last Supper with his disciples.

I reach into my tote bag to feel the silver chalice. I have come prepared with wine and wafer to partake of Holy Communion in this sacred setting. Entering the room, I feel the meaning that this place holds for me and for millions of other believers across the centuries.

I am drawn to a corner of the empty room where a shelf protrudes out from the wall. It is here that I create a temporary altar and begin the communion preparation, as I had done so many times before. I take out the shining silver chalice and pour the wine into it. I place two wafers on the small silver tray. With one of my minister friends next to me, I begin to speak those potent, life giving words, "This is my body, which is given for your sake; this do in remembrance of me... This is the cup of the new covenant in my blood which is shed for you." (Luke 22:19 & 20)

Finally, in prayer-filled reverence, I lift the wafer and the chalice and speak my own prayer of dedication. Again, I surrender my life and ministry to Christ. With this covenant spoken, I take the wafer and drink the wine and become part of the golden thread that connects me back to what was revealed in this very room nearly two thousand years ago.

There is such a mystery in the practice of Holy Communion and yet, in some ways, it is very simple. Of course, I had done it as a child in my local church. Then, for the whole middle portion of my life, it simply didn't exist in my awareness. It was as if it were some cast-off activity, like so many other things of childhood.

Within the first year of my ministry, I sensed something was missing in my spiritual practice. As I was preparing for my Easter services, I was brought back to the story of the Last Supper. So, I got some crackers and some grape juice, read the scripture story and sat at my little home altar and took communion. It simply felt right to do so.

My own version of Holy Communion came during that same year, on New Year's Eve; I was in meditation about my vision for the coming year. Suddenly, I felt impelled to re-create the communion in a new way. That evening launched a process of discovery filled with meaning and mystery. I began to work with several formats and read and re-read the Sacred Scriptures recounting that "first supper". Eventually, I developed a format that was easily incorporated into my own spiritual practice.

I began to study about it and ask for guidance to more fully understand its use and practice in my life and my ministry. I wanted to find a way that would bring "new life" into a seemingly old ritual. The first thing I recognized is that it was the last teaching Jesus gave to his disciples before his death. Somehow, that seemed significant. Sure, there were many other teachings but he saved this one for last.

I continued in the practice, although not on a regular basis.

On occasion, I would offer it in a special evening service at my church. And when I traveled to ministers' conferences, I would invite a few selected friends who were also drawn to the practice to join me in the sharing of communion.

About that same time, I reconnected with futurist and author Barbara Marx Hubbard. I had traveled to the Soviet Union with her some years before. We were brought back together through dear friends in my church, Sidney and Jean Lanier.

Actually, Barbara had moved in right down the street from where I lived. She began attending Sunday services but, most importantly, we began meditating together on a regular basis. At the end of each of these meditation sessions, we would share in communion. It was here that I began to understand its depth. Barbara and I were fulfilling the promise of God through Jesus that said, "whenever two or three of you gather together in my name, there I am in the midst of you." As Barbara and I continued in this practice, I entered into the realization of the felt presence of God. Often, we would include others in this practice, but at least once or twice a week we gathered to do it alone.

A certain pattern began to unfold in how we did it. First, the bread and wine would be prepared. Then, we would sit in the silence followed by each of us stating our "intention" for the communion. In a sense, these statements were what we were either asking to know about God's presence in our lives or they took the form of announcements about our devotion to God.

After the statement of our individual intentions, one of us would repeat the words of scripture and then we would both partake of the bread and wine.

I remember one of these sessions as if it were yesterday. We were in Barbara's living-room, which looked out over a canal, and up in the distance you could see Mt. Tamalpais. The morning sun was shining through and its light filled the room. Then, with Barbara as my witness, I stated my intention to go the whole way in Christ.

The words were strong as they flowed through my lips. They seemed to be anointed with the Holy Spirit. In saying them, I felt something change in me. And change it did.

I made a commitment to experience Holy Communion every day for a year. I sensed I had to do it as part of my daily practice to more fully understand its mystery for myself. So, as the next January approached, I began to prepare myself. I bought the wafers from a church supply store, got a beautiful chalice and dish, and prepared the place for it all near my bedside.

What you have to know is that I have made these kinds of commitments to myself before and always broken them. Even though I was engaged in a daily dedicated spiritual practice, on occasion there would be those days for whatever reason, I would be rushing out of my apartment without having done my practice. So, when I started, I truly didn't know if I could or would be able to keep the agreement I had made with myself.

Today, I can say that it wasn't always easy and some nights I did it in a hurried and distracted manner but I did, in fact, take Holy Communion every day for a little more than one year. When the year was completed, I knew something greater about myself. For that year, at least, I had gone the distance. Not only had my faith deepened but also there was something about keeping my word, my agreement to myself, that has since made a huge difference within me. Since then, there have been a few students of mine who have also committed to this same practice for a year—also with wonderful benefits.

Ultimately, it was about my relationship with God as Christ in me. Others who watched me that year later confirmed how I had been transformed. I knew something had changed and the source of the change was within. It was during that precious year that I realized—made real to myself—the truth that the real blessings of Spirit must originate in our own beingness, in our own consciousness. Transformation is an inside job.

For the next few years, I included Holy Communion in my spiritual practice, although not on a regular basis. Most often, I would return to it when I sensed that I was drifting away or was somehow lost from my center. Sometimes, there would pass several months between taking it. But there was hardly a time when I couldn't look back and feel the true accomplishment of having lived a year of my life from and within its sacred practice.

A couple of years ago, I invited it back into my daily practice. And, for most of my days, it is part of how I reaffirm my love for God.

Note that I used the word "invite." It is a practice of invitation. When I engage in Holy Communion, I'm inviting the Living Presence of God that is Christ into my life. When we partake of communion, we are really having a relationship with the Universal consciousness represented in the Christ, and we come to the awareness that this consciousness is alive in us. As we share in communion with others, we enter into this body and consciousness together and the promises of the "two or more" continue to unfold in our lives.

Here's what I have come to know. For me, the wine represents the consciousness of Christ. It is the Light and Love that worked through Jesus. It is the activity of God that has always been, is here now, and shall be forevermore. It was present at the beginning as the supreme gift of God to this creation on Earth.

Others before Jesus had been touched by this Light and Love that is the crystal-clear consciousness of Christ, many of whom we've never heard of and some of who became world teachers. But it was Jesus who was willing to go the whole way and demonstrate it for all people to come. In Jesus, Christ left the cave, the mystery school, the hidden temple, and came out into the street for all the world to see. Jesus, as this consciousness in action, was willing to leave what had previously been the closed sacred communities, and walk out into the dark consciousness of the world and show humanity the next step in its relationship with God.

And the step that he revealed was very different than what had gone before. Until this time, the Goodness of God was only possible after death in some far off place that was greater and grander than what could ever be known or experienced on Earth.

It's hard for us today in our modern world to comprehend, let alone understand, that kind of life. Granted, there are still places in the world where the only hope some people may have is that life after death will be better than the present drudgery and darkness.

But it was into that kind of world that Jesus walked out and proclaimed "heaven was at hand." And, at that time, there was little evidence and certainly less agreement, for that kind of bold idea.

That's just one of the many reasons people were afraid of him. Basically, the religious structure couldn't tolerate such upheaval.

Until that time, all the world's religious traditions sought their heaven, by whatever name they called it, "up there" and "after this." All religious practices were geared to a getting ready to "go there," "after here.."

This was changed with Jesus. He brought "there" "here". Christ is the Consciousness of Heaven that was brought to Earth through the man Jesus. Was he the Son of God? Yes. He was the person through which the Light and Love of God came to earth in a new way. But it didn't stop with him. The promise is that we are all sons and daughters of the Most High and that same Light and Love that moved through Jesus is always available, standing ready to be awakened and revealed through us.

It's been said that Buddha built a bridge to Nirvana, to the consciousness of Light and Love, but it was Jesus who walked that bridge in the other direction, towards earth, in order to bring that consciousness to humanity.

I've often said that there's as much, if not more, of the Consciousness of Christ in any given room where people are gathered in the name of God, as there was when Jesus walked the earth. This is because for two thousand years people have been inviting Its Light and Love into their lives, their hearts, their minds, and their flesh.

Back to the meaning of communion. Our next question becomes, "What about the wafer? Is it really the body of Christ?" Let me share what it represents to me. First of all, I just generally feel that it's easier to get our arms around the concept of the Consciousness of Christ. It's invisible but through all sorts of spiritual practice, we can get a sense of it, feel it, and commune with it. For many people, this first takes place in nature, like it did for me in the pine forest in Michigan. It's so easy to feel it in the silence and beauty of nature. Perhaps, this is because we can feel so small compared to the mysteries and power of nature whether it is a roaring ocean or a serene sunset. Whatever setting it might be, the door to the feeling of an intelligence or life greater than ourselves shows its face to us.

However, it's another step altogether to get our arms around the symbol of the bread. It was something that gradually worked in me, unfolding ever so slowly in my experience of Holy Communion. What I have come to comprehend is that, as the wine represents the Consciousness of Christ, the bread is the demonstration of that Consciousness in form. It is first, last, and always, heaven come to earth.

One of my first clear recognitions of this came with the understanding that the Consciousness of Christ is invisible. It is the pure essence of the Light and Love that God is. And the job of this Consciousness is to take *form,* to move from the unmanifest realm of thought to the manifest realm of form.

How and where does it take form? This is the most important question, and when the answer was given, I was transformed. It can only take form through individual consciousness. That means you and me as well as every other human being who has ever lived on earth or who will ever live here.

And it only goes where it's invited. It was as if I had been hit over the head. Christ can only take form through us.

I began the work of living with this idea and seeing that every time I took communion, I was asking Christ to enter the world through me, to be made flesh and real through me and into my experience of life.

Did my life always look like I was living in this kind of anointing? Certainly not, but I kept entering into the process and the practice, kept inviting It into my being.

Gradually, my life began to get easier. I became more prosperous and lived from a real sense of freedom that I had never before experienced.

One of the things I realized about this whole idea of Christ only going where It's invited is that I would need to begin to live my life in this same way. By this, I mean I would need to stop promoting or marketing my work or my ministry. In other words, I too would only go where I was invited. I would only go where individuals or churches called me to go. Now, let me say, that for someone whose training in the business world had been in the area of sales and marketing, this was no easy lesson!

However, I did understand something of what was happening to me. If I wanted to live from the Christ of my being it would be fruitless to go where it wasn't invited. Of course, there were times I tried, but the experience would always be of struggle and effort with little, if any, results to show from it. On the contrary, when I prayed to be taken where I could serve, the phone rang. The project or workshop would then be completed with the greatest of ease and comfort. And I would always be more than fully provided for.

Through the years of living my life like this, I know that the Consciousness of Christ has been made flesh in the lives and experiences of the many people I have been privileged to minister to, teach and serve.

What started in that upper room in Jerusalem worked its way across the centuries right into my own heart and thus into my life.

Finally, there is one other note that stems from this understanding of communion. It is this: the Second Coming is not about the return of a given person to earth. Instead, it's the revelation of the God essence come again in each and every person who has prepared their hearts and their minds and their flesh for it.

The preparation for it is not easy but I believe it is the ultimate destiny of every soul. at some time in eternity. It is the promise that speaks to us across the centuries. It is the promise of new life in the twinkling of an eye. It is the promise of being born again in any moment and under any circumstance. It is the promise of being resurrected from hate and bitterness. It is the promise of being healed from sicknesses and poverty. It is the promise of being raised up from the dead ways of living and thinking. Simply put, it is the promise of the essence of the Light and Love within Jesus Christ to be birthed into my awareness and bring Its sweet elixir of Truth into my life for now and forevermore. Nothing less would do for us, the children of God.

Christ is the consciousness (wine) that takes form through the man, Jesus (bread), and this process is continually duplicating itself within individual consciousness, within the heart where each one of us lives and moves and breathes and has our being, in order to bring more and more of what is called the blessings of heaven into the world in which we live.

This is where the practice of Holy Communion had taken me, and through it, I know why Jesus saved the best teaching for that last night in the Upper Room. We have come to call it the Last Supper. I would suggest another more appropriate name for it. I now refer to it as the "First Supper," for it was on that night in that holy room that the full mystery of heaven coming to earth was first given to those who loved Him.

And, today, in our time, the gifts of this "First Supper" are continually being given to those who love Him, to those who have been called according to His one and only purpose, which is to love. I also know that the upper room that I visited in the Holy City of Jerusalem lives eternally in each of us.

Practice:

Participate in a communion service in a church that lifts your spirits, or, if that's not possible, acquire some simple, natural bread (or cracker, or Matzoh, the unleavened bread eaten at Passover), and some wine, and design your own communion service.

Many communion services are based on the Christian belief in the Blood and Body of Jesus Christ. They are a sacrament in which consecrated bread and wine are consumed as memorials of Christ's death or as symbols for the realization of a spiritual union between Christ and the believer, or as the actual, transmuted, body and blood of the man we call Jesus Christ.

Whatever the belief, communion is a service ritual or ceremony of commitment to a spiritual union between the Christ aspect of God and an individual or group. The purpose is to have a relationship with God that is both intimate and personal. When you are in a relationship with Christ you are sharing with Him and He is sharing with you the Holy Spirit as the Presence. The experience is true Oneness.

As you take in the bread and the wine, contemplate what it means to take in Jesus' "body and blood," and how you may be transformed by this experience.

Chapter 10: Peace

The Poolside Mass
Puerto Vallarta, Mexico

Near the serene azure pool, secluded by palm trees and vibrant green foliage, the Sunday Mass is about to begin. I had read the announcement on my way to breakfast and knew I wanted to attend. When I arrive, the attendants are setting pristine white linens on the altar. The sparkling brass candle holders are then added, along with the multicolored fresh flowers. It seems as if the glory of God is being made real on this simple table of the Lord.

The priest, Father Tony, walks around and introduces himself to each of us.

His warm "hello" and radiant smile open the hearts of our little group. Though not a Catholic, I welcome this special time when I can be quiet and turn my awareness home to God.

Father Tony begins the mass in gently, flowing English with intermittent Spanish phrases. The sun filters through the palm trees as he speaks of the Peace of Jesus being upon us. He proceeds to repeat the idea of Jesus' Peace being with us.

I remember that it was only a few weeks earlier that I had declared "peace" to be my purpose for the New Year. Father Tony continues to weave this theme throughout the service. Yes, the Peace of Jesus is real for me at this very moment. I am being lifted up through the glow of this realization. A feeling of comfort enters my awareness as I give thanks for the profoundness of this simple service that will forever alter my experience of this vacation. I also give thanks for the many times I have found peace and tranquility in Catholic churches around the world.

I've always loved being around the water and my years of synchronized swimming shows brought me great joy. I had a friend whose family had a swimming pool and we spent most of the summers in the water. When we went to high school, we participated in developing water shows for family and friends at the new high school we were attending. After high school, I attended college and participated in two years of water shows. After that time, I had the opportunity through a professor to travel to Europe for several weeks with others who had joined the group. Wow! It really opened my eyes for understanding other cultures. Somehow, I knew then that I would travel the world.

Here, now, near this water, with these reminders from the priest, I feel the Peace that is our nature flowing in and around me.

Peace is something we all seek, not realizing that it's right here, right now. Whenever adversity enters our lives, our human tendency is to immediately react in some self-defeating manner, or to simply 'stew in our suffering' until our problem eventually resolves itself, one way or another. However, there is a better way to deal with the misfortunes of life, and that is to stop thinking about our problems and to start thinking about God instead.

This simple practice was called by Emmet Fox, the wonderful New York minister of Depression years who gave us many books to ponder, the "Golden Key" of self-transformation. It is the means by which we can create a "Peace that passes all understanding." (Phil. 4:7)

In other words, it is a Peace that is not dependent on outer conditions. Instead, it is a Peace that comes from inside out of us to miraculously change the conditions and circumstances of our lives.

It's taken many years but I've learned that the key to developing such peace is to have a simple plan that we can rely on in the face of adversity. Such a plan is the means by which we turn our desperation into the inspiration that will bring newness into our lives.

We can each create our very own Peace Plan by simply developing a list of the 'Top Ten Ways' we could be thinking about God, instead of our problems. These ways are the qualities that we think of when we are feeling God's presence. You can see that this plan is unique to each of us, and can only be developed on the basis of our own understanding and personal experience.

The spiritual principle from on which we build our personal peace is known as the universal 'Law of Worship,' which is simply stated as: *Whatever we worship we become.* This means that, whenever we give the Divine our full attention, by thinking about God instead of our problems, we tend to become like God.

Furthermore, the scriptures tell us that God is Love, and Love is the 'awareness of oneness that changes all things for good.' In other words, Love changes them for the better, and forever. Consequently, whenever we begin to think about God instead of our problems, our problems begin to change into something good through the power of God's Love that flows from the inside of us outward.

To experience Peace, therefore, we must attend to it. And, just as a single snapshot could not show us a whole house, likewise a single description could hardly capture the whole essence of the spiritual experience of Peace. Therefore, we can only come to understand the nature of Peace by looking at it from as many different views as possible.

Over the years, I've found many wonderful descriptions of Peace. Following is a short collection:

"Peace I leave with you, my peace I give
unto you: not as the world giveth, give I unto you.
Let not your heart be troubled,
neither let it be afraid." - Jesus Christ [John 14:27]

"Because God is Peace and because God is in you,
the Peace of God must also be in you.
You should no longer go in search of Peace,
for this is confusion....
Peace is brought about through a conscious unity
of our personal being with the inner principle of our
life — that underlying current, flowing from a divine
center is pressing ever outward into expression in
our lives." ~Ernest Holmes

"Peace comes from within you
Do not seek it outside of yourself." ~ The Buddha

"We look forward to the time when the Power of Love
will replace the Love of Power.
Then will our world know the blessings of peace."
   ~William Gladstone

"Peace is always beautiful." ~Walt Whitman

Let there be peace on earth... and let it begin with
me." ~ The Peace Song by Jesse Colin Young

"From the cradle to the grave a person never does a
single thing which has any first and foremost objective, save one – to secure peace of mind, spiritual
comfort for themselves." ~Mark Twain

"The Lord will keep us in perfect peace,
when our mind is stayed on Him." ~Isaiah 26:3

"Peace cannot be kept by force. It can only be
achieved by understanding." ~Albert Einstein

"You are a radiator of health, harmony and peace
if you love this law: God is the strength of my heart."
~Emma Curtis Hopkins

"Nothing can bring you lasting peace but the triumph of Principles." ~Ralph Waldo Emerson

"If there is to be peace in the world...
there must be peace in the heart."   ~Lao Tse

"Heaven is not a place where we go when we die,
it is the peace we recieve when we choose to love."
   ~ Lloyd Strom

"Peace is the harmony and tranquility derived from an awareness of the Christ consciousness. Steadfast affirmation of peace will harmonize the whole body structure and open the way to attainment of health conditions in mind and body."   ~Charles Fillmore

"Better indeed is knowledge than unconscious action.
Better than knowledge is meditation.
But better still is the surrender of attachment to results, because what follows is immediate peace."
~Bhagavad Gita (12:12)

"The fruit of Silence is ...Prayer;
The fruit of Prayer is ...Faith;
The fruit of Faith is ...Love;
The fruit of Love is ...Service;
The fruit of Service is ...Peace." ~Mother Theresa

By considering how each one of these individuals 'sees' the nature of Peace, we will begin to develop a more holistic view of what Peace really means.

Now, to worship something is simply to give it our full attention. So we must remember that worry is a form of "problem worship." Consequently, whenever we worry, we tend to become like our problems, instead of what we want to be, which is something good, like God. Therefore, I've learned to focus my attention on my "Top Ten Ways" of thinking about God instead of my problems. I've learned that, in doing so we must, by the Law of Worship, become the Peace we seek.

Practice:

Repeat this prayer for peace of mind:
Be still and know that I am God, I am the Christ, the Light of the Living God within me. I am the Principle of Peace within me. I am the manifestation of Love within me. My mind is poised in Peace and Beauty. All sense of fear and doubt is gone, I rest in calm trust and rely on the Law of Spirit to bring good into my experience of Life.

I contend with none, argue with none, and am filled with wonderful Peace and Light There is no uncertainty about my future and no fear as a result of my past I live in an eternal Now which is filled with good alone. Goodness and Beauty follow me, Happiness and Wholeness fill my entire being with the realization of Love and Perfection.

I am the Christ, Light of the Living God within me. This inner mind of mine is now Divine and complete. It has no worries and no fears. It is whole, complete and satisfied, I look back over all previous experience and find that it was good, very good, I look toward the future and find that it is good, very good. I look at the present and find that it is also good, and very good, God is in all, overall and through all

I am the Christ, Light of the Living God within me, I am the Spirit of Confidence. I am poised in Love and Reason. I am the perfect Law of Truth and the complete Presence of Beauty*

I am Christ, Light of the Living God within me.

*From *The Science of Mind* by Ernest Holmes, pages 264,265

Chapter 11. Love

The Ashram
Rishikesh, India

The sun is glistening on the river as I make my way under the huge archway and pass through the gate of the ashram. My awareness comes to rest on my breath as I speak a prayer of thanksgiving for all that has transpired to bring me to this ashram at the foothills of the Himalayan Mountains.

It's my last morning in India. My feet carry me to the white marble steps that descend down to the great Ganges. I'm walking on the very steps that have brought swamis, sages, devotees and pilgrims to participate in the rituals and worship practices associated with this sacred river.

I glance toward the mountains and back to the water. It's truly a glorious day. My eyes stop their wanderings and focus on an elderly couple at the water's edge. They are performing their morning ritual of washing and praying at the river. I'm watching as brown skin, worn with age, and white hair, crowning a lifetime of promises, move before me. My whole being feels drawn into their sacred practice of removing their clothes, washing their bodies, and putting on fresh clothes all with great modesty.

Completing his washing, the man turns to face the flow of the river. He stands there, silently raising his hands to the center of his chest in the traditional position of prayer. Shortly, the woman finishes, and reaching into her bag, she takes out bright fuchsia flower petals and gently tosses them as her offering into

"Mother Ganges." Then, she turns and kneels before her husband and touches his feet

I watch this sacred exchange between beloveds. How many acts of surrender have brought them to this love-filled peace? How many struggles have their lives endured? How much pain have they given to this river during a lifetime of togetherness?

It seems it's all passing too quickly, for they are now finished and begin packing their belongings. I am not complete. There is more to be given from this moment beyond time. As they turn to leave, our eyes connect and quiet smiles of recognition pass between us. They walk up toward the top of the steps where I am sitting. The woman, now moving with the support of a cane, approaches me and reaches out her frail and wrinkled hand. I respond and accept it into mine.

Then, with my tear-stained lips, I gently kiss it. Love and devotion pour from the center of my heart. I have traveled half way around the world to this land of India to know once again, as if for the first time, that we are all One in the great river of God's flowing love.

India is one of the most diverse countries I've ever visited. The expansiveness of the Himalayan mountains coupled with the great Ganges River opened my heart once again. The saris the women wore were filled with such color and beauty; I never got tired of watching them walking through the streets and doing their morning ablutions at the river's edge.

Practice:

I do a process of healing that was given to me by Spirit while I was on a Ministry Retreat. I was directed to re-

call every person in my life from the moment I was born then thank them and forgive them or myself for the involvement in my life. I also praise them and raise them in the name of Christ. The first day I did the practice I spent 8 hours remembering people. I have spent many hours since that time doing this practice... Funny thing is I keep remembering people.

> *If I were to be asked directly as to the quickest way for a person to get their healing power going, I would probably say, 'Praise everything and everyone in your mind, and as far as your mental convictions will demonstrate promptly, speak these praises aloud.'* ~ Emma Curtis Hopkins

I Praise My Feelings ...I've Raised My Feelings ...I Feel Like Christ.

I Praise My Vision ...I've Raised My Vision ...I See Like Christ.

I Praise My Hearing ...I've Raised My Hearing ...I Hear Like Christ.

I Praise My Speaking ...I've Raised My Talking ...I Speak Like Christ.

I Praise My Praying ...I've Raised My Praying ...I Pray Like Christ.

I Praise My Actions ...I've Raised My Actions ...I Act Like Christ.

I Praise My Loving ...I've Raised My Loving ...I Love Like Christ.

I Praise My Wisdom ...I've Raised My wisdom ...I Am Wise Like Christ.

I Praise My Wholeness ...I've Raised My Wholeness ...I Am Whole Like Christ.

I Praise My Healing ...I've Raised My Healing ...I Heal Like Christ.

I Praise My Giving ...I've Raised My Giving ...I Give Like Christ.

I Praise My Acceptance ...I've Raised My Acceptance ...I Accept Like Christ.

I Praise My Freedom ...I've Raised My Freedom ...I Am Free Like Christ.

I Praise My Life ...I've Raised My Life ...I Live Like Christ.

*I Praise My Being ...I've Raised My Being ...I Am Like Christ.**

*Perfect Praising Prayer, by Lloyd Strom

Chapter 12: Joy

The Cave

Patmos Island, Greece

    I begin to feel the holiness of this place as I walk down the narrow winding steps that lead me deep into the stone opening known as the Cave of the Apocalypse. Entering the darkness of the cave, sprinkled only by the soft golden glow of the burning candles, I find a place to sit. My elbows rest on the high side-arms of the straight-backed chair that was designed to support a monk during long hours of praying and chanting.

    Bowing my head, I begin to give thanks for the journey that has brought me to this special place. A silent prayer begins to form... "Beloved St. John, hear my prayer that your joy may be made full within me." I continue to repeat these precious words until they encircle the rhythmic pattern of my breath and become written on my heart. There is a growing intensity in the prayer until, finally, it tapers off into silence. I have no idea how long I've been sitting here.

    Occasionally, a few other tourists enter my awareness as they quietly come and go from the Cave. I'm alone again. My focus moves to the headrest St. John used that is a few feet from where I'm sitting. It was carved out of the stone in the cave wall. I get up and walk over to be near it. I give thanks for his Gospel. It has been a blessing and inspiration to my life.

    I'm standing right where Jesus appeared to St. John and gave him the words that would become The Revelation, the last book of the Holy Bible. Blessed John, the beloved disciple whom Jesus loved and in whom the joy of Christ was made full. I have journeyed to this beautiful island in the Aegean Sea seeking only to know and experience the promise of such joy.

"...that your joy may be made full within me." These very same words had been heard here before, perhaps many times across the centuries. Now I share them with you, knowing that what was written so long ago continues to be alive with meaning for us today.

I feel St. Paul's anointing of Love upon my heart. It is this gift of Love that is continually extended to all of humanity through the Loving Presence of the Living Christ. Just as St. Paul said, "... which is Christ in you, the hope of glory." (Colossians 1:27)

As I contemplate these memories, I'm filled with God's Grace and Love. I now know the joy of serving others only brings back more joy into my life. May you all be blessed by what you give to others in the name of Love.

Practices to Ease the Way

The following practices have been developed over the decades for my work and for my students. They have proved very helpful for all of us.

Spiritual Mentor

A 'Spiritual Mentor' is a wise and trusted guide though life, who functions as both a teacher and advisor on spiritual matters alone. A 'mentoring session' should always be a one-on-one interaction, where we learn to apply the universal Principles of Truth to the unique situations in our own lives.

It is important to consciously acknowledge the Mentor-Student relationship, so that an opportunity for a valuable lesson in life is not engaged as a casual conversation. This is most effectively accomplished by an exchange of financial consideration for the Mentor's time. This can take place in the form of an 'appreciation offering,' or a mutually agreed upon fee. Either way, it graciously establishes a right relationship between the Mentor and the Student, and places value upon their interaction.

Prayer Partnering

Prayer partnering is a way to support yourself and another person. Set up a dedicated time to connect and share weekly what is going on in your spiritual life as well as the Joys and trials and tribulations of daily life in the world. Sharing your most deeply held thoughts, joys, worries, and desires is a freeing experience. Praying with another person validates our ongoing growth and connection with Spirit.

Make sure to choose a partner that lives in Truth.

Writing A Sacred Covenant

A Sacred Covenant is, quite simply, a conscious courting of Christhood by intention. The framework around which a Sacred Covenant is formed includes a "purpose," a word that we desire to reveal in our lives as the Truth of our being. It also includes a "vision" statement describing the activity of Spirit that will reveal this purpose. All of this is then sanctified by a sacred or inspired quote (often from the Bible) as a "for it is written" authority.

A Sacred Covenant is a practice and a tool which, when performed genuinely and authentically, becomes more than a mere agreement, it becomes Accord, restoring the Holy Bond of Creator and creation. In this way, our own stated intentions reflect THE Word, not your own.

Starting A Christ Circle

The Christ Circle practice is a high and exalted expression of the "two or more gathered in His Name." A group of four or five is a good size for a Christ Circle. It is an arena of Love and Trust where the human personalities involved can be put aside exposing the inherent Christ and union with Immortal Mind Presence.

A Christ Circle includes prayer, sharing, inspired readings, confession and surrender to the Silence.

In many ways, a Christ Circle replicates an essential practice that the Apostles engaged in during their earthly ministries. They would often gather together in an "upper room" consciousness to rejuvenate and vitalize their souls among other kindred spirits in restoration of Holy Memory, the "blood and body" of Jesus Christ.

A Christ Circle, when engaged in rightly, can announce the meekness and poverty of spirit the Master spoke of so many times by exhibiting Truth in its participants.

An Uplifting Treatment[2]

I SEE YOU, __(name)__ , above, transcending your past. I see you unweighted, free; I see you as complete Spirit. Nothing can be added to you; nothing can be taken from you. I see you as health. You are one with universal health. Nothing can spoil universal health. It is God putting away disease. I see you as omnipotence. Nothing can defeat omnipotence. It puts aside weakness and shows me God working before me for you, and through you, and by you, for ever and ever.

You face me as God, unweighted, unattached, unspoiled for ever and ever. I see you as wisdom looking toward me to speak by you of your heavenly wholeness and peace. I see you as peace. I see you facing me as peace that the world cannot take away. I see you as peace putting aside discord. God is showing peace now with its touch on your outer life at every point. You are free God becoming visible for my sake, that Truth may prevail.

By the grace of God Almighty—by the grace of the Holy Ghost—by the grace of Jesus Christ now falling upon you and working in you, I command you to show yourself to all the world as untainted health and free omnipotence from this day forth.

---

[2] By Emma Curtis Hopkins, who taught and ordained Charles and Myrtle Fillmore, printed in the May, 1933, issue of *Daily Word*

An Uplifting Treatment for Oneself[3]

I SEE ME, __(name)__ , above, transcending my past. I see me unweighted, free; I see me as complete Spirit. Nothing can be added to me; nothing can be taken from me. I see me as health. I am one with universal health. Nothing can spoil universal health. It is God putting away disease. I see me as omnipotence. Nothing can defeat omnipotence. It puts aside weakness and shows me God working before me for me, and through me, and by me, for ever and ever. I face me as God, unweighted, unattached, unspoiled for ever and ever. I see me as wisdom looking toward me to speak by me of my heavenly wholeness and peace. I see me as peace. I see me facing me as peace that the world cannot take away. I see me as peace putting aside discord. God is showing peace now with its touch on my outer life at every point. I am free God becoming visible for my sake, that Truth may prevail.

By the grace of God Almighty, by the grace of the Holy Ghost-by the grace of Jesus Christ now falling upon me and working in me, I command me to show myself to all the world as untainted health and free omnipotence, from this day forth.

---

[3] By Emma Curtis Hopkins, who taught and ordained Charles and Myrtle Fillmore, printed in the May, 1933, issue of *Daily Word*

Prayer of Acceptance

If you have any concerns about your ability to experience something that you feel called to be or do, use this prayer to accept that which is constantly being provided by the Consciousness of Christ.

There is only one Life.
This Life is good; this Life is God; this Life is my Life now!
I know that this Life is a source of Infinite Intelligence, acting in me, through me, and all around me.
And even though I may not know how to provide the means to _____, I know that this Intelligence knows exactly how to provide everything necessary for me to be and do all that is mine to be and do.
Therefore, I fully accept the physical and financial means that are so graciously provided by the Presence of the Christ in me.
I now release any thought, belief, idea, attitude or suggestion that I might hold that does not support my experience of _____.
As I accept this Good into my life, I give thanks with an open, gracious and joyous heart.
Amen.

Prayer of Reconciliation

I have forgiven you.
You have forgiven me.
I have forgiven you.
You have forgiven me.
I have forgiven you.
You have forgiven me.

You and I are one in God.
I love you. You love me.
You and I are one in God.
I love you. You love me.
You and I are one in God.
I love you. You love me.

I am grateful to you:
You are grateful to me.
I am grateful to you.
You are grateful to me.
I am grateful to you.
You are grateful to me.

There is no longer the slightest
ill feeling between you and me.
I pray for your happiness
from the bottom of my heart.
May you be blessed with
increasing happiness.

Thank you very much!
Thank you very much!
Thank you very much!

About the Author

In the mid 1990s, Rev. Marcia left a growing and vibrant pulpit ministry in Northern California to pursue a 'new form of ministry' that would serve the revelation of Christ in humanity. Her previous career success in higher education and then in business provided the foundational skills that would lead her to consulting and working with ministers and church leadership teams. She has facilitated thousands of people in the advanced application of the Principles of Universal Truth through retreats, classes and public appearances. She has also served as a Spiritual Mentor to many of the leading ministers in the New Thought movement. In addition, she has traveled to more than 45 countries and leads tours to sacred sites around the world. She ministers and teaches from the 'Sacred Days Sanctuary' in Portland, OR.

Acknowledgments

I'm grateful to the many hundreds of students who shared with me their courageous steps toward greater self-realization. It was always an honor and privilege to stand witness to the Light in each of them.

I'm grateful to my Initiates for whom I have served as Spiritual Mentor and to all the people who attended the "Sacred Days" retreat programs. I'm also grateful to those devoted students who I was able to guide through their Ministerial Ordination process. My faith was deepened and expanded through all of our work together.

I have been graced by the church congregations in California and Oregon that I served as Senior Minister. Each of them, in their own unique way, taught me more about how to love. I'm also grateful for the many ministers and churches who opened their doors and their hearts to my work and invited me to facilitate some of their most important healings.

In addition, I'm grateful for the many members of the Christ Circles who come together each week to practice seeing with the "eye of the heart." They have taught me so much. I'm grateful to my beloved Metaphysical Bible teacher, the late Rev. Dr. Paul Barrett, and to the presence of Rev. Suz Ogden in my life. She has enriched my ministry through her gift of song.

I'm filled with love for the Revs. Catherine Pena, Christine Green, Marjory Dawson, Karen Gifford, Kathy Hearn, Marianne Fitzpatrick and Mark Vierra, who joined me for the 'long road' of this journey. I'm forever appreciative to them for their love and willingness to grow together with me in the "Revelation of Christ."

I continue to be deeply and richly blessed by my long association and collaboration with the Rev. Lloyd Strom. His unfailing love, guidance and wisdom have made all the difference in my own journey and in my ministry.

Finally, I'm eternally grateful for my departed parents, Marvin M. Sutton and Marjorie E. Pung, who I will honor, bless and love throughout all of our lifetimes to come.

Gratitudes from Students & Colleagues

Marcia has been my minister, teacher, mentor, friend and traveling companion. She taught me spiritual practices that enhanced my soul's journey to know who I am and Whose I am. She opened my eyes to welcome the Living Christ into my life. I am eternally grateful to her. ~ *Rev. Marjory Dawson*

I first got to know Marcia when she was in ministerial school and interned with me at Pacific Church of Religious Science in San Diego. Through the years the student became my teacher and ushered me across countless thresholds of awakening and healing. Marcia's love and teachings are my daily companions, my high tower and the essence and substance of my support of others. I am grateful beyond words. ~ *Rev. Dr. Kathy Hearn*

On our 2009 journey to Israel I really began to know you as an incredible person and teacher. You quoted Holmes, Hopkins, and Steiner with such ease as you taught. I kept asking questions, and one day you said, find a friend and read Emma aloud together then you'll really learn and understand. And so I did, and I will be eternally grateful for your guidance, insight and teaching. You are a blessing to your students and humanity. Thank you! ~ *Rev. Eileen Brownell*

The first time I saw Rev. Marcia, she was a guest speaker at a local New Thought Church. From the moment she started to speak, my soul opened. Her words touched a part of me that had been closed for so long. That was almost 30 years ago and to this day her words still hold a special place in my heart. Thank you, my Beloved Friend, for all we share in Christ. ~ *Rev Char Terranova*

Remembering that day I felt and knew I would have a relationship with Rev. Marcia before I met her as she walked down a hallway toward me. She became my teacher and friend. She is a compassionate woman who was always ready to know the truth about you and pray for you. Marcia's view of the Universe is wonderfully creative and she brings that belief to all her teaching. She opened my heart to my potential, teaching the deepest healing is a receptive heart and the deepest gratitude is a life lived in devotion to the presence of love, Jesus Christ. ~ *Rev. Karen Joy Gifford*

My dearest Marcia and I have been in each other's lives for over 36 years. We first met in Practitioner training in 1984 and then went through ministerial school, graduating together in 1989. Marcia opened the glorious path to "Finding the Christ" which was her favorite chapter in the SOM textbook. She has played difference roles in my life through out these many years and the most precious to me is our loving friendship. She has inspired so many and opened the heart and minds of a multitude in a variety of ways with her teachings and wisdom. As I was typing this to add to the book for her, amazingly...she called me. As always, we ended the call saying we love each other, and so too ...I will end this writing with "I Love You Marcia". Thank you for all you gave to me and so many, many others that have been Blessed to know you dear one. ~ *Rev. Marianne Fitzpatrick*

From the first class I attended of Marcia's, I was intrigued with her clarity, wisdom and conviction. She possessed a light and presence that inspired me. I am deeply grateful for her wisdom as a teacher, a mentor, a pilgrimage leader in our travels and most of all for her friendship. She empowered those around her to share the tools and resources she created and thousands have been lifted by her work. We are so blessed. ~ *Rev. Christine Green*

Through spiritual practices, I began seeing with the 'eye of the heart' the false beliefs in my subconscious and moving from fear to faith. Classes, retreats, and pilgrimages taught me to recognize, realize, and reveal the presence of Christ within and see the Christ in others. I am eternally grateful to you as my minister, teacher, and friend. ~ *Rev. Mary V. Haines*

It is so difficult for me to share the life experiences I had with Rev. Dr. Marcia Sutton. We traveled, prayed, laughed and even sung together. She was my teacher in how to be and not to be. I will always be grateful for all the lessons and blessings I inherited from her. We still have a laugh once in a while and we are always glad to stay in touch. For me she was the great expression of human and divine. ~ *Rev. Dr. SuZ Ogden*

In every generation, there are those precious few who selflessly offer the transmission of Wisdom and Truth to spiritual Initiates. I know in my heart, and from my personal experience with her teachings, that Marcia is among these exalted souls. I have been honored over the years to claim her as mentor, teacher and friend. The Presence of the Christ in Marcia has been a Light, a touchstone and an inspiration to me, and many like me that has served as a true blessing and a gift. ~ *Rev. Dave Luce*

My first experience of Marcia was extremely transformational and I immediately became her student. She quickly introduced me to the power of spiritual practice, the Christ within, the deeper meaning of sacred scriptures, and new rooms in consciousness. Her light, love, wisdom, deep and grounded prayers have blessed my life beyond measure. I am eternally grateful and committed to live as love as she taught me. ~ *Rev. Dr. Penny M. Macek*

I have had extraordinary experiences with Marcia over the years. When Marcia summarized a teaching point or complex thought she'd say, "The bottom line is ..." So the bottom line is she brought me to Christ. It changed me forever.

Thank you Marcia. My eternal Love and Gratitude in Jesus Christ. ~ *Rev. Catherine Dollahite*

Publishers Note

In the 90's Marcia gave up being the minister at the Religious Science Church in Sausalito, California and moved to Portland. My wife Char and I were 2 of the 4 students in the first class she taught in the Northwest, I was totally amazed at her presence. I thought, "this woman has more God than anyone I have ever met." What I did find out is that she is more able and willing than anyone I have met to let God teach and speak thru her.

I thought I was a minister before I met her. Little did I know the amount of growth and understanding of Spirit that were to come from this relationship. I consider Marcia to be my spiritual mother. I feel like I grew into being a minister because of her presence in my life. I studied with her for over fifteen years. She wrote this book in 2012 but decided not to publish it then. In 2019 I asked her if I could publish it. She said she would add some words to it so I could publish it.

I own WiseWoman Press and publish all the works of Emma Curtis Hopkins as well as other current ministers. Marcia taught two classes on two of Emma Curtis Hopkins' books and I was hooked on Emma's works. Then Marge Flotron, who had been publishing Emma's works, passed on and I wanted more of Emma's books. I thought Marcia and Lloyd Strom would publish the books. No way, so I decided to find a way to publish the books. Ruth Miller and two women started WiseWoman Press to publish Ruth's *Unveiling Your Hidden Power,* and after they had published some other titles I joined. They moved on and I finally became the owner of WiseWoman Press, and it is an honor to be able to publish this.

Marcia taught the presence of Christ and opened me to the Truth of Christ. I am happy to see this book be in the hands of dedicated spiritual believers. Her trip through The Journey to the Eye of the Heart is truly "Christ Awareness" and will inspire many to seek the Truth of Christ

Blessings and Love on your Journey
~ Rev. Michael Terranova, publisher
WiseWoman Press

Books Published by WiseWoman Press

By Emma Curtis Hopkins
- *Bible Interpretations: Series I thru XXII*
- *Class Lessons of 1888*
- *Drops of Gold Journal*
- *Esoteric Philosophy: Deeper Teachings in Spiritual Science*
- *First Lessons – from the 1887 journal*
- *Genesis Series 1894*
- *The Gospel Series*
- *High Mysticism*
- *Judgment Series in Spiritual Science*
- *Resume*
- *Self Treatments including The Radiant I Am*

By Ruth L. Miller
- *Unveiling Your Hidden Power: Emma Curtis Hopkins' Metaphysics for the 21st Century*
- *Coming into Freedom: Emilie Cady's Lessons in Truth for the 21st Century*
- *Power Beyond Magic: Ernest Holmes Biography*
- *Power to Heal: Emma Curtis Hopkins Biography*
- *The Power of Unity: Charles Fillmore Biography*
- *The Power of Thought: Phineas P. Quimby Biography*
- *The Power of Insight: Thomas Troward Biography*
- *The Power of the Self: Ralph Waldo Emerson Biography.*
- *The Power of Practice: Emilie Cady Biography*

By Frances B. Lancaster
- *The 13th Commandment*
- *Abundance Now*

By Cath DePalma
- *I Can Do This Thing Called Life – and So Can You*
- *Energize Your Creative Super Powers*

By Ute Maria Cedilla
- *The Mysticism of Emma Curtis Hopkins*
  - *Volume 1 Finding the Christ within.*
  - *Volume 2 Realizing the Christ, One in All*

www.wisewomanpress.com

www.ingramcontent.com/pod-product-compliance
Lightning Source LLC
Chambersburg PA
CBHW022134080426
42734CB00006B/357